CHRIST PREEMINENT

A Commentary on Colossians

Alden A. Gannett

kregel
PUBLICATIONS

Grand Rapids, MI 49501

Christ Preeminent: A Commentary on Colossians

Copyright © 1998 by Alden A. Gannett

Published in 1998 by Kregel Publications, a division of Kregel, Inc., P.O. Box 2607, Grand Rapids, MI 49501. Kregel Publications provides trusted, biblical publications for Christian growth and service. Your comments and suggestions are valued.

For more information about Kregel Publications, visit our web site at www.kregel.com.

Scripture quotations are primarily from the King James Version of the Bible. The author includes interpretive word changes and literal renderings from the original languages.

Cover design: Alan G. Hartman
Book design: Frank Gutbrod

Library of Congress Cataloging-in-Publication Data
Gannett, Alden A.
    Christ preeminent: a devotional commentary on Colossians / Alden A. Gannett.
        p.   cm.
    Includes bibliographical references.
    1. Bible. N.T. Colossians—Commentaries. I. Title.
BS2715.3.G36   1998   227'.707—dc21   97-41093
                                                                    CIP
ISBN 0-8254-2730-4

Printed in the United States of America

1 2 3 / 03 02 01 00 99 98

To my lifelong sweetheart,
Georgetta,
who daily lives the truth
that is taught in Colossians:
"Christ in you,
the hope of glory."

Contents

Foreword

When it comes to physical food, this is a day of great plenty for many of us. Fast-food restaurants and diners can be found on almost every commercial corner. Supermarkets are located near most neighborhoods, and the aisles are bursting with good things to eat. Or you can pick up the phone and order anything from pizza to Chinese food.

Yet when it comes to spiritual food, we live in a day of famine. Many centuries before Christ, the prophet Amos spoke of such a famine. And in our day we are witnessing a trend away from solid Bible teaching—a trend toward replacing biblical exposition with devotional thoughts, bite-size truths, and practical principles with little or no biblical foundation.

For more than fifty years, Dr. Alden Gannett has been serving up spiritual food in nutritious portions. I have been privileged to hear him teach God's Word many times. In fact, as the president of Southeastern Bible College, where I received my foundational biblical training, he became my spiritual mentor and good friend.

I am especially delighted that, after many years of preaching and teaching on the preeminence of Christ, Dr. Gannett has extended this ministry to the printed page. This book contains a carefully constructed blend of solid biblical insights from the text of Colossians; personal anecdotes and stories from the author's years of ministry; and pointed, practical applications designed to get the Word beyond our minds and into our lives.

If you have heard Dr. Gannett preach, you will recognize his familiar style. If you have not heard him, you will be delighted with his unique, refreshing approach to serving the appetizing meat of God's Word.

Most of all, this is a book written by a man deeply in love with Jesus Christ. I urge you to read and carefully reread *Christ*

Preeminent and find your love for the Savior rekindled and strengthened.

Don Hawkins
Cohost/Producer, *Back to the Bible*

Preface

The seed for this book was planted in my heart years ago by a Dallas Seminary professor, when he exhorted us in his class to read a book of the Bible through many times.

In response, I was led by the Spirit to the Book of Colossians, which initially I read thirty times, each time at one sitting. In so doing, I fell in love all the more with our wonderful Lord, who taught me that Jesus Christ is not only to be my Savior and Lord but also to become my very life. Paul wrote: "When Christ, who is our life, shall appear, then shall ye also appear with him in glory" (Col. 3:4).

Through the years, I have preached this epistle many times in churches and in Bible conferences, and while doing so I have grown in appreciation of the fact, as we shall see, that Colossians is a book on the spiritual life.

My purpose in writing, therefore, is not primarily to provide another technical and scholarly work on this timely epistle. Rather, my aim is to set forth a practical word by expounding the theme of the epistle—the preeminence of Christ in our daily walk.

I trust that the reader will appreciate and appropriate more than ever the truth of Colossians: Not only are we saved by grace, but we also live by grace. The Christ who died for us on the cross and saved us by His grace now lives within us by His grace. Only when we understand this, can the Risen One indwelling us indeed become preeminent in all we do and say, to His praise and glory.

As we study this life-transforming truth in the Book of Colossians, I pray that we will more and more give our glorious Lord the preeminent place in our lives.

Chapter 1

INTRODUCTION TO COLOSSIANS
(1:1–14)

There is no more timely book in all the Bible than the Book of Colossians. In our day, as in Paul's, the church is continually agitated and plagued with false teachings, especially with regard to the person and work of Christ. Satan lied to our first parents in Eden, and he has been lying ever since.

I understand that agents of the Federal Bureau of Investigation are given specialized training to recognize counterfeit hundred-dollar bills. Instead of studiously examining the counterfeits, they handle many thousands of the real thing and thereby become thoroughly familiar with the genuine bills.

At Colosse, false teachers were endeavoring to supplant the truth of the gospel, as Paul calls it, with counterfeit doctrines such as humanism and legalism. Recognizing these threats to Christianity in the city of Colosse, Paul undertakes to expose the believers to the centrality and preeminence of the "real thing"—the Lord Jesus Christ.

You and I are living in a day when all across our land we are getting away from the preeminence of Christ. Too often the Holy Spirit is given the supreme place of the Lord Jesus Christ, and that is wrong. Gimmicks are taking the place of the Lord Jesus Christ, and that is wrong.

We are minimizing the doctrine of the person and work of Christ, and that is wrong. We are getting off on tangents. We seem to have to talk more about which version of the Bible to use than about the glories of our blessed Lord. That is wrong!

God wants, through the Book of Colossians, to bring us back to the centrality of our Lord Jesus Christ—who He is, what He did for us on the cross, and how He wants to live in and through us. In two words, Christ preeminent.

Let me introduce the setting of the book. We are impressed with two reasons for Paul's writing this epistle: his response to the greetings from the church at Colosse through Epaphras and the report of the danger threatening the church, called by Lightfoot the Colossian heresy.

This heresy was both doctrinal and practical. It was doctrinal in that the Colossians were substituting inferior and created beings (angels) for Christ Himself. It was practical in that they substituted meats and drinks, Sabbath laws, the rite of circumcision, Greek philosophy, pride, and will-worship for the believer's completeness in Christ.

Paul's answer is the supremacy of Christ and His sufficiency for the believer in Christ.

W. Graham Scroggie concludes, "A true Christology is the final answer to every heresy that ever has been, or ever will be."[1] Thus we study Colossians with its theme, the preeminence of Christ.

Salutation (1:1–2)

Let us read what God has to say to us in Colossians: *"Paul, an apostle of Jesus Christ by the will of God, and Timotheus our brother, to the saints and faithful brethren in Christ which are at Colosse: Grace be unto you, and peace, from God our Father and the Lord Jesus Christ"* (vv. 1–2).

Paul is the author. Timothy, a dearly beloved coworker, joins with Paul in sending his greetings.

Paul states his authority. He says, I am an "apostle." The reason is that the backdrop of the book is what we call the Colossian heresy. Doctrinal error was knocking on the door of the Colossian church. Some people were stirring up a pot of humanism (as it is called today), a pot of legalism, mysticism, and asceticism, endeavoring to rob Christ of His glory and His all-sufficiency.

Epaphras, having come from Colosse, shared this burden with the apostle Paul in Rome. Paul responded by writing to the Colossians about the preeminence of our Lord and His all-sufficiency. He wanted the saints at Colosse to stand fast, which they were doing at the time Paul wrote. But he did not underestimate the enemy of our souls.

So instead of calling himself "a servant," as he did in many other epistles, here Paul calls himself "an apostle." With authority he writes this eternal, inerrant Word, to minister Jesus Christ to people who are subject to false teaching. By the Word it is possible to come through triumphantly and victoriously.

Notice, Paul says he is an apostle "by the will of God." This is very important. It is essential that you and I be where we are, doing what we are doing in "that good, and acceptable, and perfect, will of God" (Rom. 12:2).

If you have any doubt about that, spend extra time in the Word. Spend extra time in fellowship with God's people. There is nothing like being in God's will and nothing better than the privilege of doing God's will. I love the affirmation of the psalmist: "As for God, his way is perfect" (Ps. 18:30). And it is great to be in that perfect will of God.

Paul's greeting in verse 2 is *"to the saints and faithful brethren in Christ which are at Colosse: Grace be unto you, and peace."* This is not just a formality, like hello or good morning. Paul wanted the Colossians to know that the overflowing grace of God was available to them. He wanted them to experience the glories of the peace of God that passes all understanding, about which he wrote in Philippians 4:7, by appropriating that grace through faith.

So as we study the Word and are reminded that by faith we appropriate that grace, I trust that more and more we will experience God's wonderful grace.

Thanksgiving (1:3–8)

A word of thanksgiving appears before Paul's prayer for the Colossian Christians: *"We give thanks to God and the Father of our Lord Jesus Christ, praying always for you, since we heard of your faith in Christ Jesus, and of the love which ye have to all the saints, for* [because of] *the hope which is laid up for you in heaven"* (vv. 3–5a).

What a model church! The great triad of Christian maturity characterized these believers at Colosse—faith, love, and hope. They had faith in Christ Jesus. Isn't it beautifully simple?

That is how they entered the family of God—by faith. "For by grace are ye saved through faith; and that not of yourselves: it is the gift of God: not of works, lest any man should boast" (Eph. 2:8–9).

Have you come to the Lord by faith, confessing in the words of the hymn writer, "Nothing good have I whereby Thy grace to claim"? You realized that you were an unworthy sinner before a holy God. But you learned from the Scriptures that Jesus Christ, God's Son, died on the cross for your sins and that on the third day He was raised from the dead according to the Scriptures. Having heard that glorious news, you trusted Christ to save you.

Have you done that? I hope you have trusted Him, that you now have an appetite for His Word, and that you love the things of Christ. If so, thank God. But if you have never done so, there is no better time than now.

The gospel is being preached across the world. Therefore, the Lord could come today. Do not wait any longer. Bow your head and pray, "Lord, save me." If you mean that prayer from your heart, He will! For the Bible says, "Whosoever shall call upon the name of the Lord shall be saved" (Rom. 10:13). I invite you in the name of Jesus to trust Him—right there, right now.

The proof that the Colossians had trusted the Savior, verse 4 goes on to say, was that they had love for "all the saints."

Are there any saints you do not love? There was a woman in Birmingham, Alabama, who talked about saints and "the saints." "The saints," according to her, are the unsaintly saints! They claim so much, but they are worldly and indifferent. They are wayward and out of fellowship with the Lord where real joy is made full.

Do you have love for all the saints? Do you Baptists love the Presbyterians? Do you Presbyterians love the Methodists?

These Colossians loved *all* the saints. Is there a brother or sister you cannot look in the eye? Do you have an unforgiving spirit or a wrong attitude toward anyone? Then go to that person or write a letter, and see that the matter is made right with him or her, as well as with God, so that when the Lord comes you do not have to apologize to someone. Do you love all the saints? I trust so.

All of this, Paul goes on to say in verse 5, is "[because of] the hope which is laid up for you in heaven." These people believed in the return at any moment of our Lord Jesus Christ. They were relatively new Christians, but they knew of the blessed hope of the Lord's return.

One time I was speaking on 1 Thessalonians 4 about the Lord's return, and a pastor came to me after the service and said that he had been preaching in his church for ten years and had not started preaching on the Lord's coming yet. What a disappointment! He was ten years too late getting started, according to Paul.

These Colossian believers had been saved probably only a year or two, but they knew about the Lord's return. They were looking for the imminent coming of the Lord Jesus Christ, eagerly anticipating it. In fact, according to our text, they had faith in Christ and love for all the saints *because of* the hope that was theirs. I trust that this hope is yours today.

The doctrine of the Lord's return is especially precious to me, because I was saved through this teaching. How wonderful! The Spirit of God dealt with my own heart when I was seven years old. My mother was a faithful Bible teacher who loved the Lord and loved the Word of God. She took the Scofield Correspondence Course from the Moody Bible Institute, and learned for the very first time that Jesus Christ could come back at any moment—perhaps today.

I had not murdered anybody and had not robbed any banks, but I knew I was a sinner and that I was not ready for the Lord to come.

In that context, one evening after Mother had taught us again and again at the supper table about the Lord's return, she said, "Son, your father and I are going uptown. We'll be right back."

Well, they went uptown, but they did not come right back, and I thought the Lord had come and left me behind. I was terrified! Tears gushed down my cheeks, because I was fearful that the Lord had come and I was left to go through the awful tribulation period of which the Bible speaks. Thank God, my parents' car did come down the road, and I had another opportunity to be saved—as you do now.

I did not sleep much that night; I could not eat breakfast the next day; I could not eat lunch. Mother was very sensitive to the fact that something was going on in my heart. So after father, brother, and sister had slipped away, I said, "Mother, tell me once more how to be saved." She said, "Son, God loves you. Christ died for you. If you'll trust Him, He will save you."

I bowed and prayed these very words: "Lord Jesus, I trust *You* to save *me*," and I meant them with all my heart. That moment, the guilt was gone. The burden of sin was gone. The joy of the Lord came into my heart, and it has been real ever since.

Are you ready for the Lord to come? You have been saved and you know it, and you are sure of it? Your sins have been forgiven? You have life in Christ? The joy of the Lord is your strength? You have trusted our wonderful Savior?

The Colossians had faith in Christ and love for all the saints because of the hope that was theirs.

Paul further describes his readers in verse 6. This gospel *"is come unto you, as it is in all the world; and bringeth forth fruit, as it doth also in you, since the day ye heard of it, and knew the grace of God in truth."*

These Christians at Colosse not only had faith in Christ and love for the Lord's people and their confidence in that blessed hope, but also they were continually bearing fruit. Indeed, they had the real thing.

When I taught at Dallas Bible College years ago, our school was small enough for the graduating students to give their testimonies in chapel. By the way, that is a good witness. Wherever I preach, I purpose to give my testimony. I learned that from Peter and Paul. And you too should give your testimony and do it often.

The seniors in the school would give their testimonies, saying that at one time God had dealt with their hearts and saved them and that they had grown in the grace and knowledge of the Lord. Then they said that sometime later they backslid and floundered for a while, but subsequently God restored them to precious fellowship with Himself, and they came to Bible college to train for the Lord's work. That kind of testimony was repeated over and over.

Hearing that, I sat there and said, "Lord, does it have to be like this?" Then I found my verse—Colossians 1:6. These Colossians had continued to bear fruit since the day they knew the grace of God in truth. That is the key.

Continually the Colossians bore fruit. They walked in fellowship with the Lord, sharing Christ, exercising their gifts, ministering to God's people with a word in season where there was need. God was wonderfully using them. Again, what a model church! What a fellowship of God's people!

This paragraph concludes with verses 7 and 8: *"As ye also learned of Epaphras our dear fellowservant, who is for you a faithful minister of Christ, who also declared unto us your love in the Spirit."*

On the basis of this verse, we can say that probably Epaphras was the missionary-evangelist who came from Ephesus to evangelize and to plant the church in Colosse. Having heard the burden about the Colossian heresy, Paul wrote this letter and sent it back with Epaphras.

You will notice that Paul wanted to know something about the progress of the church at Colosse. Paul was saying to Epaphras as he visited the apostle in prison, "Brother Epaphras, tell me about your church. How are things going in Colosse? What characterizes your fellowship more than anything else?" In verse 8, Epaphras replied, "Brother Paul, it is their 'love in the Spirit.'"

That is the new commandment John spoke about in his epistles. It is the love Paul taught in 1 Corinthians 13, fellowship characterized by love in the Spirit. Is that the characteristic of your church? I trust that it is. I trust that this is the characteristic of all of us, that we will grow in this grace of fervently loving one another with pure hearts (1 Peter 1:22).

Prayer (1:9–14)

After Paul's thanksgiving, he records his prayer for the Colossians beginning with verse 9: *"For this cause we . . . pray."* For what cause? That they had faith in Christ and had love for all the saints because of the hope that was theirs and because they were continually bearing fruit from the very day they "knew the grace of God in truth" (v. 6).

For whom should I pray? (1:9)

You pray for sick people, don't you? Of course you do, and you will keep on until the Lord comes. You pray for someone who has lost a job, for someone who has special needs in the family, for a home with tensions, for a loved one on drugs. Burdens are shared for people who are lost. I trust that you remember all such particular needs.

But Paul here is praying for people who were well spiritually, for Spirit-filled Christians. He is not praying about problems, in terms of their walk with God. He is praying for people who were walking with the Lord. This point is important: We are to pray not just for people who hurt and have special needs but also for those who are walking with God, who are in fellowship with the Lord, that they will remain that way and keep growing in the Lord.

Recently my wife's heart and mine were saddened as two people who were ministering the Word of the Lord in the past had difficulties. Their home was broken. It grieved our hearts. They were not continuing to grow in grace and in the knowledge of our Lord and Savior Jesus Christ.

Every one of us knows some people who used to be in church, who used to share the time of prayer, who used to gather together for worship and to celebrate the Lord's Supper. But today they are missing. They do not want to be there. Do you now see the people for whom Paul prayed?

So let us keep on praying for the sick and those who hurt and those who have special needs, but let us not forget those who are walking with God today—that they will continue to do so and for His glory alone.

For what should I pray? (1:9)

Paul's specific request is in verse 9: *"For this cause we also, since the day we heard it, do not cease to pray for you, and to desire that ye might be filled with the knowledge of his will in all wisdom and spiritual understanding . . ."*

Very simply, Paul is saying, "Lord, fill them full of the Word." That is where God's will is found—in the Word. So much of it is already written in the Book, is it not? Lord, fill these growing Christians with the knowledge of Your will in all "wisdom and spiritual understanding."

All of us have asked, "What shall I buy my loved one for Christmas? Or what can I give for a birthday gift?" One day my wife said that about one of our daughters-in-law. It is simpler to put a check in the mail, she concluded. What do you buy for someone who has everything?

Also, what do you give to people who *have* faith in Christ and love for all the saints and enjoy that blessed hope? What do you do for them? Paul answers, you should pray for them that they will be increasingly filled with the Word of God.

I have made my living by studying, preaching, and teaching the Word for at least fifty years. But the more I study it, the more I realize that I must study it. The more I learn, the more I realize what I do not know, and the more I want to learn the glorious riches of grace in Christ Jesus.

So we pray for people who are walking with God, for people who are leading us in spiritual things. We pray for their growth in our precious Lord: "Lord, fill them full of the Book in all wisdom."

There is a difference between knowledge and wisdom. Knowledge is information. Wisdom is the application of knowledge.

We used to live in London, Ontario, where we served with the London Bible Institute, or LBI, as it was then called. One day our children were playing ball between our house and the neighbor's house. These houses were very close together. You could just drive a car between them. And there it was that our children were playing ball.

In years past my father was a florist, and I had repaired glass in greenhouses a thousand times (I am not exaggerating very much!). So I rushed out where the children were playing before a ball could go through our or a neighbor's window, and I shouted, "Keith, don't you know that your ball could go right through one of those panes of glass? Go out into the street and play." It was a safe, dead-end street.

Would you believe it, the next afternoon those same children were there again. I could hear the crack of the bat. I rushed out again, hoping to keep the ball from breaking a window, and shouted, "Keith, didn't I tell you just yesterday not to play ball here near these houses?" He said, "Dad, we're not playing ball. We're hitting stones!"

What did Keith have? Knowledge? Yes, knowledge. But what did he lack? Wisdom, the application of knowledge. As we study the Bible, I trust that there will be the application of truth, that we will come before God in the light of the Word and claim it, and that we will make it ours in the name of Christ.

The next phrase is "spiritual understanding." We must be taught the Scriptures by God the Holy Spirit. Just lecturing will not suffice, nor will preaching alone suffice. God must work the truth into our lives. Paul desires that God will bless His Word, that there will be people saved, that all of us will grow in the grace and knowledge of Christ because there is spiritual understanding as we study the Word of God.

To what end should I pray? (1:10)

"Lord, fill them full!" To what end? *"That ye might walk worthy of the Lord unto all pleasing"* (v. 10). That is a beautiful, simple statement of the acme of Christian living—walk worthy of the Lord.

How do I find out what is worthy of my Lord? I find it in the Book. By reading the Bible, studying the Bible, meditating on the Bible, I find out what is worthy of Him, even to the point of anticipating what pleases Him. Paul says, "I want to anticipate what pleases my wonderful Lord."

My wife knows how to please me. I usually leave home for ministry on Saturday and return on Thursday. If she wants to cook something special for me when I come home on Thursday night for supper, you won't believe what it is—*spaghetti!* I love it. It's more delicious to me than a T-bone steak.

And what pleases my Lord? He has already written it down in the Bible from Genesis to Revelation. I trust we will love Him more as a result of our study in Colossians and that we will know more, each ensuing day, how to please our Lord more and more.

How do I walk worthy of the Lord? (1:10–14)

The walk that is worthy of the Lord is expressed in four specific ways in verses 10–14. The first one is that we will be *"fruitful in every good work."* You and I are to be fruit-bearing Christians. And according to John 15:5, those who abide in Him bring forth much fruit.

"Being fruitful in every good work," our text says, is not just preaching a sermon or teaching a Sunday school class. Being fruitful also includes being an effective mom or dad in the home or being grandparents (we are at that stage now). We are to be fruitful on the job, or bearing testimony for Christ to the family next door or a testimony to a student at the university.

"Fruitful in every good work? How do we become that, Brother Gannett?" Paul has already told us: by being filled with God's wonderful Word. As we study, we will see how we can become more fruitful in practical ways for the glory of God.

The second way a walk that is worthy of the Lord is expressed is also in verse 10. It is characterized by our ever *"increasing in the knowledge of God."*

How do we do that? The same way we fell in love! I fell in love with my sweetheart about fifty-five years ago. I thank the Lord for that, especially in these days when there are so many broken homes.

How did I get to know her better? I went to the right school, a Christian college. I tell young people to go fishing where the fish are, and that is what I did. I found a dedicated Christian girl at a Christian college.

To see this girl and to meet her was to love her. Instead of buying ice cream or a soda after a basketball game, we would go for a walk. Sometimes it was bitter cold, and she was dressed for it, but I was not. Would you believe it, one night it was so cold that my ear and my nose froze, and I did not even know it. That is love, brother! But we really got to know each other better because we spent time with each other.

How do I get to know my God better? By spending time with Him. Pray tell, how do you do that? He speaks to us in the Word. Did He speak to you this morning? Or last night? Whenever we have our quiet time, He speaks. And you and I speak to Him as we pray. We spend time with each other. You young people know about this, don't you? That is how we get to know our God better and better.

The third way we can please our Lord the more is mentioned in verse 11: We are *"strengthened with all might, according to his glorious power."* I used to claim this phrase for my preaching, until I read the rest of the verse. It does not talk about preaching at all. It talks about *"all patience and longsuffering with joyfulness."*

What is patience? F. F. Bruce says it is steadfastness in the hour of trial.[2] And who doesn't have trials? What is longsuffering? Steadfastness in the hour of opposition when people malign, speak evil, drag our name in the mud.[3]

Then comes the whipped cream on top of the strawberry shortcake, *"patience and longsuffering with joyfulness."* Paul says that by the grace of God you and I can be patient when we naturally desire to be very impatient with people and longsuffering when we feel like giving them a piece of our mind. Instead, we have longsuffering and the joy of the Lord through it all. That is shouting ground, isn't it?

"Where in the world do you get those virtues, preacher?" Paul has already told us. If we are filled with the Word, we will walk worthy of the Lord, and the result will be patience.

Did you hear that, Mother and Dad, when the children act like their father? Pastor with people? Your employer with you, his employee? Your neighbor? Your kid brother? With whomever, here is grace to be patient and grace to be longsuffering—with joyfulness.

Finally, we are to walk worthy of the Lord by ever *"giving thanks unto the Father"* (v. 12). Why? What has He done? *"[He] hath made us meet* [fit] *to be partakers of the inheritance of the saints in light."* Take note of that wonderful truth. If you are saved by God's marvelous grace, in Christ you are fit for the inheritance God has for you. We have a lot of growing in grace to do, but in terms of our position in the courts of heaven this hour, we are fit for the inheritance. That is exactly what the text says.

Then we are to thank God *"who hath delivered us from the power of darkness"* (v. 13). Before you and I were saved, we were children of the devil (1 John 3:10). We were on the road to hell, to eternal destruction, to eternal separation from God. That is what the Bible says a sinner is, and what his or her destiny is before coming to Christ and being saved. But thank God, when we became Christians, He saved us from all that!

And our text goes on to say that He *"hath delivered us from the power of darkness, and hath translated us into the kingdom of his dear Son: in whom we have redemption through his blood, even the forgiveness of sins."* Once a child of the devil, now a child of God. Once headed for hell, now headed for heaven. Once loving sin, now hating sin. Once ignoring the Lord, now loving Him, walking with Him in precious fellowship.

So when we are filled with the Word and therefore walking worthy of the Lord, we are ever giving thanks to the Father. We have a heart filled with thanksgiving to God for who He is and what He has done and for all that is before us in the glory. We will be with Him, we will be like Him, and we will be restored to our loved ones forever and ever! I tell you it is great to be a Christian! And Paul, filled with the Word and praying that his readers would be, thanks God over and over for the grace of the Lord in them.

Filled with the Word! Filled with the Word! This is what God wants to do in your life and in mine. How does it take place?

Application—The Four A's

W. H. Griffith Thomas years ago shared with me "Four A's" that have helped me understand how to fulfill what we have just read.[4]

The first A is *attention.*

That is what you are doing right now. You have set aside other things that you could have been doing and have given your attention to the Word of God. I commend you.

The second A suggested by Dr. Thomas is *application.*

We saw it in our text, filled "in all wisdom and spiritual understanding" (v. 9). The Holy Spirit wants to apply the truth as we share it together. We purpose by God's grace to do it. He can do it for you as you read Colossians. He may apply many things to you that He has not given to me in many hours of studying Colossians. It is wonderful what the Spirit of God will do for you.

Application! I know your wife needs it, I know your husband needs it, I know your children need it. But God is talking to *you* and God is talking to *me.* And together, by God's grace, we want the Holy Spirit to apply His Word. "It's me, it's me, it's me, O Lord, standing in the need of prayer," says the spiritual we have heard and sung for so many years.

Dr. Thomas suggested a third A: *aspiration.*

By that he meant pray over it. Sometime today we should pray over this very message. We should ask God to make it real in our lives, as well as in the experience of others.

We can do all that, but there will be no change unless we experience the fourth A: *action.*

Action says, "I am guilty of the sin that God's Spirit has brought to my attention from His Word. I don't love all the saints. I don't live by faith as I should. I don't live in the light of the any-moment return of Christ. That's not my lifestyle. I have to confess that to God." Action is confessing such sins and forsaking them.

Action is also claiming the grace of God for the truth God gave me afresh. "Oh, I need to spend more time in the Word. Lord, I claim Your grace not to let my schedule become so cluttered that I neglect the Word of God. Lord, I claim your grace to be diligent and faithful reading, studying, meditating, memorizing the Word of the Lord so that I am 'filled with the knowledge of his will, in all wisdom and spiritual understanding.'" Action!

My fellow Christian, do you have a daily quiet time? I know your schedule is busy; so is ours at our house. But we make time for what is most important, don't we? There is nothing more important every day than meeting God in His Word.

Dad, do you gather your family around the Word of God? Do you read the Bible together as a family? Do you pray together as a family? Dad, take the lead when you are home. I know that many dads are on the road, as I am. But do take the lead whenever you can. Have family worship.

You are in a good, gospel-preaching, Bible-teaching, missionary church, aren't you? You are not letting your children be given liberal teaching, are you? You are not getting only husks Sunday after Sunday from a liberal preacher, are you? You cannot grow that way. You will starve to death. Spiritually speaking, you are under the Word, aren't you, and going to a church where you are fed the riches of grace in Christ Jesus?

I know a certain pastor who said when he saw the people coming out of a liberal church that they were like animals that go to be fed but there was no food in the trough. Yet they go back. They go the second time to be fed, and again there was no food. They go back. But the third time, they do not go. However, some people keep going back although they are starving to death spiritually and starving their families, because they are not taught the Word of God.

Thank God, you want to hear God's precious Word. You want Christ to be the center and to have the preeminence in your life and in your home. That is the purpose Paul had in mind when he wrote to the Colossian Christians, and it is essential if we are to be growing in our knowledge of the Lord. This is where a life of spiritual understanding begins.

WHAT WE
BELIEVE
(1:15–2:3)

I ignore the Bible if I do not believe it, and I order my life accordingly. When I do not accept the ethics of the Bible, I am oblivious of a heaven to gain or a hell to shun. Abortion is no problem. Lying to my neighbor or cheating on my taxes is no problem if there is no such thing as truth—the Bible.

A pastor's son-in-law daily joined his friends at a bar on his way home from work, believing that a few social drinks give zest to life.

In the process of time, his wife, his father-in-law, and many others in the church kept praying and sharing the Scriptures with him, until this son-in-law became persuaded that Christians have the real thing—true life in Christ. The Bible teaching changed his life.

So it is that when we believe that the Bible is the Word of God, and I trust that you do, then we will obey its precepts. If we believe that Jesus Christ is the Son of God, the one and only Savior, and that He came and lived a perfect, sinless life and then died on the cross for our sins and rose again the third day, that requires responsibility, doesn't it?

We are to become right with our God who is our Creator, Sustainer, and Redeemer and then live soberly and righteously and godly in this present age. We are to practice what we believe.

Keep in mind that the Colossians were being attacked by false teachers who had come to persuade them that Christ is not God, that He is not the one and only Savior, and that we need not bow before His authority. Instead, they urged, mix together a humanistic philosophy, legalism, mysticism, and asceticism. This, they taught, is the "superior" knowledge they claimed to possess in terms of a person being right with God.

Facing the issue of false teaching at Colosse, Paul counteracts it with truth. He begins with doctrine—the person and work of Christ.

This is a day when many people minimize doctrine and say that it is not important. I will never forget the time I attended a Sunday school class in Oklahoma taught by a teacher from the local university. I was startled as I heard her say, "Let's get rid of doctrine." *Doctrine* is another word for *teaching*. A school teacher was unwittingly pleading, "Let's get rid of teaching."

Since the Bible is the inerrant Word of God (that is, it contain no errors in the original autographs), and it claims to be, I had better find out what it says, what it means, and how it applies to my daily living.

You and I live in a world riddled with false teaching, a world that substitutes humanistic religious philosophies—what humans think—for what God has written in His inerrant Word.

I trust that as we study this Book of Colossians, we will more and more have our minds and hearts saturated with truth, so that we will know what error is. We will be prepared when Satan subtly brings it our way through some television or radio preacher, some book or magazine, or some cult member who comes and knocks on the door of our home.

In short, Paul begins the heart of his epistle with doctrine, the teaching of God regarding the person and work of our Lord Jesus Christ. So let us call the first section of this letter (Col. 1:15–2:3) doctrinal. Paul follows this foundational portion of his epistle with what has been called the polemical section (2:4–3:4), in which he directly confronts the error at Colosse.

The final division, the hortatory (3:5–4:6), is the application of the truth to the believer's life.[1]

The Person of Christ (1:15–18)

Christ's relationship to the Father (1:15)

We begin with doctrine.[2] In verse 15, Paul, speaking of our Lord Jesus, says He *"is the image of the invisible God."* God is Spirit, isn't He? Christ is the One who brought God down to earth and made the invisible One visible to us. For He is the image, affirms Paul, the derived likeness of God Himself.

This sounds like John 1:1, "In the beginning was the Word [Jesus Christ], and the Word was with God, and the Word was God." So, John's gospel also declares that Jesus Christ is God.

In John 10:30, our Lord said, "I and my Father are one." This affirms the deity of our Lord Jesus Christ. And in John 14:9, He said, "He that hath seen me hath seen the Father." Deity! This is the language in Colossians 1. The Lord Jesus Christ is the image, the derived likeness, of the invisible God.

We have one daughter and three sons in our family. Mother and daughter were shopping in Philadelphia some years ago. The salesman interrupted his own sales pitch and said, "Excuse me, please. It is obvious that you two are mother and daughter. Will you tell me why one of you talks like a Yankee and the other talks like a Southerner?" A derived likeness.

There is a synonym in the original language that means an accidental likeness, like that between apples and peaches. They are both fruit, yet distinct.

But Jesus Christ is a derived likeness, the very stamped image of God Himself. And Paul says to these Colossians, when error was knocking on the door of their church, "Jesus Christ is more than a good man. He is more than a great teacher. He is God, very God." It is here where he begins his doctrinal teaching—with the full deity of our Lord Jesus.

If you take that out of your Bible, you rip your Bible to shreds. If you do, close your church and go home and do your own thing, for if Christ is not God, then He is not true. He is a fake. Christianity is not the true religion. Salvation is not available through the shed blood of Christ. He never arose from the dead. He is not coming again. He is a mere man. That is what these false teachers were teaching.

But our text teaches that He is God! Jesus Christ's relationship to God the Father, first of all, is His oneness with the eternal Father; He is God's eternal Son.

Christ's relationship to the creation (1:16–17)

Notice now Christ's relationship to the creation. Verse 16 affirms, *"By* [in] *him were all things created."* This statement follows the close of verse 15, where Paul makes the great affirmation that Jesus Christ is *"the firstborn of all creation,"* as the New Scofield Bible translates it.

If you have not had the cult members knock on your door yet, you will soon. They are in the business of a worldwide propagation of their false teachings. They teach that Jesus is a mere creature—greatest of all the created beings but a mere creature. They claim that Colossians 1:15 tells us so: Christ is "the firstborn of all creation."

The term *firstborn* gives us the key. It was the term used in Old Testament days of the eldest son, who had a unique position in the family. If the father died prematurely, the eldest son had the responsibility for his mother and his younger brothers and sisters until all were grown and cared for.

The reward for this was that he received double the inheritance. If the deceased father had four children and five acres of ground, the eldest son received two acres whereas each of the other children received only one. Thus the eldest son had a unique position in the home.

The Holy Spirit through Paul, using that analogy, begins verse 16 with the explanatory conjunction *for.* The Scripture states plainly, *"For by him* [literally, in him] *were all things created, that are in heaven, and that are in earth, visible and invisible, whether they be thrones, or dominions, or principalities, or powers—all things were created by him, and for him."*

Then Paul delineates what that unique position is in God's creation. What does verse 16 say? "All things were created by him, and for him." Note that Paul adds, "He sustains all things." Jesus Christ's unique position in all God's creation is that He is the Creator and Sustainer of the universe! How could He be a created being if He is the Creator Himself?

Do not ever forget this text. You will need it one of these days, when two nicely dressed people will knock on your door and invite you to believe their error, and they will try to use the Bible, this very verse, to prove their denial of the deity of our Lord Jesus Christ. Watch for it!

Let us pause here a moment. Verse 16 affirms, "By [in] him were all things created." Paul says Jesus Christ is the Designer of God's creation. The Designer! Did you know you are designed by God? Did you ever look in the mirror and thank God for what you see there?

We have a dear friend who was a pastor. His fifteen-year-old daughter, who had definitely professed Christ as Savior, took her dad's gun one Saturday night at home and put two bullets into her head. She was not satisfied with God's creation.

She spent all the money she could on clothes, hoping they would improve her self-image, but that did not satisfy her. She is in heaven today because she had trusted Christ, but she was not satisfied with God's creation. Are you?

A lot of people suffer from a poor self-image. According to verse 16, I am to look in the mirror and thank God for what I see. Although we see people around us who are far more beautiful or handsome, we are nevertheless the creation of God. He gave us our intelligence, our personalities, our gifts, our talents—all are from Christ. That makes you somebody, because the Lord God of heaven designed you.

Jesus Christ is the Designer. He is also the Agent of creation. All things were created by Him, things we can see and things we cannot see. All across God's universe, everything was created by God. Genesis 1:1 states, "In the beginning God created the heaven [the sun, the moon, and the stars], and the earth." The myriad of stars were created by God. Adam and Eve were created by God Himself. So were you and I.

If you have a problem with creationism versus evolution, let me try to help. The issue is whether the Bible is the Word of God or not. Since the Bible is the Word of God, the issue is settled in Colossians 1:16.

This is precisely what John 1:3 declares: "All things were made by him; and without him was not anything made that was made."

Colossians 1:16 then adds, "All things were created by him, and for him." That too makes you somebody in God's sight. Our Lord not only designed you and created you, but also He created you for Himself—for His glory.

Do you and I live daily for the glory of God? Do we begin each day desiring to live it for God's glory alone? Paul wrote to the Philippians, "Christ shall be magnified in my body, whether it be by life, or by death" (Phil. 1:20).

We are to live and serve to the glory of God. Anything less than this, according to the Bible, is idolatry. When something else is first—girlfriend, boyfriend, husband, wife, job, sports, church—if anything is more important to you and me than the Lord Jesus Christ, we are idolaters, according to Exodus 20. It is as though we had bowed before a graven image.

Will you let God give you this text now, as I ask Him to give it to me anew? We are the creation of God. He designed us. He created us for His glory. That is what life is all about.

In verse 17 Paul goes on to say, *"And he is before all things."* He cannot be a created being and antedate all things. Then the apostle adds these words, *"By him all things consist."* As Dr. H. A. Ironside penned, "It is His hand that holds the stars in their courses, directs the planets in their orbits, and controls the laws of the universe. How great is His dignity, and yet how low did He stoop for our salvation!"[3]

Perhaps you have seen the Moody Institute of Science film, *God of the Atom,* portraying so vividly that there is an invisible power, the Second Person of the Godhead, who holds together the ingredients of nuclear energy.

You may remember or you have read about World War II, when the atom bomb was dropped on Hiroshima. In Los Alamos, the atomic bomb and hydrogen bomb were created. It is no wonder that the enemy did not discover that it was being developed out there in the middle of nowhere. The last I heard, our government is spending 500 million dollars photographing the atom going through a tube 500 yards long. If the scientists had just read Colossians 1:17, they could have saved over 500 million of our tax dollars.

The Bible tells us that the atom is the creation of God. The invisible power that so many scientists do not understand is the power of the Second Person of the Godhead, the Creator, our Lord and Savior Jesus Christ.

Christ's relationship to the church (1:18)

In verse 18 Paul turns to the new creation, the church, the body of Christ, and adds this glorious word that our Lord is its head. Paul continues, *"And he is the head of the body, the church: who is the beginning, the firstborn from the dead; that in all things he might have the preeminence."*

Christ is the head of the body. The New Testament in this very text teaches that the church is the body of Christ, and this church universal is expressed in local assemblies (or churches), with our Lord as its head.

When I went to school, they told us that when we put our finger on a hot stove, the finger did not move until the message was communicated to the head; then the message was returned to the finger telling it to move fast! We have all experienced this. The head directs the body.

Just so, Jesus Christ, the head of the church, gives direction and leadership to His body composed of born-again believers from Pentecost to the Rapture. He is the head of the body. Therefore I must bow my knee to Him. I am to worship Him as the living head of the church. He does not reside in Washington, nor in Moscow, nor in Rome. He resides at the right hand of the Father. He is the supreme head of the church.

Paul goes on to say in verse 18, "Who is the beginning [that is, the source of the church]." He is *"the firstborn from the dead."* Others have died and have been restored to life, but only our Lord Jesus Christ is the first in resurrection from the dead to receive a body that will never die again. So He has that unique position of being the first in resurrection, for He is the living head of the church.

To what end? Paul concludes verse 18, "That in all things he might have the preeminence." He insists that Christ is God, very God. So He is worthy of the first place. "Why preeminence, Paul?" He has the unique position in all creation. "Why first, Paul?" He is head of the church, the body of Christ, "that in all things"—not some things, not most things, but in all things—"he might have the preeminence."

I ask you as you read this: As far as you know, in the presence of God, is Jesus Christ first in your life? Business is not first. Family is not first. Fishing is not first. Christ is first in your life.

According to the Scripture we have just read, Jesus Christ is Lord of the *old* creation. As more and more people are being saved by His grace, He is becoming more and more Lord of His *new* creation, the church. Is He your Lord? If not, I invite you now, before we go on to the next paragraph, to bow and acknowledge the lordship of Jesus Christ over everything in your life.

The Work of Christ (1:19–23)

In relation to the Father (1:19)

We turn now from the doctrine of the person of Christ to the doctrine of the work of Christ, beginning with verse 19—the glorious doctrine of reconciliation. *"For it pleased the Father that in him should all fulness dwell."* This verse is normally interpreted by Colossians 2:9, "In him [Christ] dwelleth all the fulness of the Godhead bodily."[4]

But the contexts are different. Therefore I suggest, with S. Lewis Johnson, that this is the teaching of verse 19: It pleased the Father that in Christ should all saving fullness dwell.[5] I mean that in eternity past the three Persons of the Godhead consulted. The Father planned it all, determined the future of planet earth and the universe. He knew when He created humans innocent in the Garden of Eden that they would fall.

So the blessed Trinity planned for a Reconciler. Jesus Christ agreed to come to planet Earth, to die for our sins according to the Scriptures and be raised again the third day according to the Scriptures (1 Cor. 15:3–4).

Therefore our Lord could say in John 14:6, "I am the way [to the Father's house in heaven], the truth, and the life: no man cometh unto the Father, but by me."

Peter could say in Acts 4:12, "Neither is there salvation in any other: for there is no other name under heaven given among men, whereby we must be saved." Our salvation is only through Jesus Christ, God's Son, who died on the cross and rose again for us. So Romans 3:25 speaks of our blessed Lord: "Whom God hath set forth to be a propitiation [satisfaction] through faith in his blood." This is God's one way—the only way—of salvation.

Has God opened the eyes of your understanding to this truth yet? Or do you think that you are saved because you were baptized as a baby? Or that you will go to heaven because you were confirmed as a young person? Or because you joined your church?

The chairman of our board in Birmingham, Alabama, testified on one occasion, "At the age of forty, I thought I had my salvation all bought and paid for."

You may have lived a good life. You may be a good father, a good husband. You may earnestly endeavor to do what is right and honorable before God and man. None of these is the issue. Have you bowed as a sinner before the Son of God, the one and only Savior who died for you and rose again, and have you called on His name to save you? Have you ever done that? Can you remember when?

I can tell you the year I was saved. I was seven years old. I regret that I did not write the date in my Bible. I hope you will, if you remember it. I do not have the date to treasure, but I can surely take you to the place, my home, where I entered into the human family, and then entered the divine family at a later time. I can take you to the place.

Are you that definite about your salvation? Is there no question in the world that if Christ were to come today you would go to be with Him because you are saved and you are certain about it on the authority of God's written Word? Or do you just think so, hope so? Can you sing, "Blessed assurance, Jesus is mine"?

Many church members are going straight to hell because they have never bowed as sinners before the Savior and trusted Him for their salvation. If you have never done that, do it before you go on to the next paragraph.

Jesus Christ's relationship first to the Father, as we saw in verse 19, makes Him the one and only Savior.

In relation to the creation (1:20)

Christ's relationship to the creation is seen in verse 20. *"And having made peace through the blood of His cross, by him to reconcile all things unto himself; by him, I say, whether they be things in earth, or things in heaven."* Notice Paul's reference to things. He gets to people in a moment. Here he writes about reconciliation of things. Why things? Because God's universe had been tainted by sin.[6]

Regarding the object of this reconciliation, Robert G. Gromacki very clearly expounds: "In verse 20, reconciliation is first applied to the universe ['all things'; 1:20]. It incorporates the scope of the created world ['whether they be things in earth, or things in heaven'; cf. 1:16]. The universe became unclean through angelic and human sin [Job 15:15; 25:5]. The world of plants and animals suffered damage because of the sin of man [Genesis 3:17–18; Romans 8:19–22]. Christ died to purify both heaven and earth [Hebrews 9:23]. The benefits of His death will be manifest to this total domain in the millennium and throughout the eternal state."[7]

In relation to the church (1:21–23)

Heretofore, Paul has been discussing the work of Christ in relation to God the Father—in His role as Reconciler—and subsequently, in His work of reconciliation of all things unto Himself. Now he personalizes His work even more as he relates Christ's work of reconciliation to his readers, the church—people (v. 21). *"And you* [the believers at Colosse], *who were once alienated and enemies in your mind by wicked works, yet now hath he reconciled."*

Notice that Paul describes his readers before they were saved. They were aliens from God—*estranged* from God is the term—enemies, hostile in mind by wicked works. Hence, it is not true that everybody is going to heaven, that all religions lead to heaven. Not for one moment, according to the Bible!

I've heard it said, "Preacher, I've never clenched my fist in the face of God and said, 'I'll have nothing to do with You.'" You do not have to. Jesus said, "He that is not with me is against me" (Matt. 12:30). All you have to do is say to God, "Thanks, but no thanks." "God, I don't care what You say in the Bible. I don't believe that Jesus Christ is the Son of God. I don't believe He is the one and only Savior. I'm not even sure there is a heaven or a hell. Thanks, but no thanks." If you say that, it is clear that at this moment you are not a Christian.

However, thank God, you do not have to remain in that spiritual condition. If you will now acknowledge your need for Christ's death on the cross as final payment for your sins, because you are estranged from God and hostile to God by your wicked works, and then trust Christ to save you, He will do just that for you, now.

Application: God's glorious provisions (1:20–2:3)

If you will trust the Savior to be yours, there are four glorious provisions accomplished by His reconciliation.

Peace (1:20)

Look first at verse 20. Christ *"made peace through the blood of his cross."*

At this point we must pause and ask, Did we not see above the emphasis in verse 20 upon the reconciliation of "all things"— the universe? Indeed we did. We must clarify. In the context of this verse, the reconciliation of things is defined as "things in earth or things in heaven." Significantly, Paul omits the phrase of Philippians 2:10, "and things under the earth" (better is the NASB, "of those . . . under the earth").

Warren W. Wiersbe explains, "It is likely 'under the earth' refers to the lost, since God's family is either in heaven or on earth (Ephesians 3:14-15). One day all will bow before Him and confess that He is the Lord. Of course, it is possible for people to bow and confess today, and receive His gift of salvation (Romans 10:9-10). To bow before Him now means salvation; to bow before Him at the judgment means condemnation."[8]

John Eadie adds a helpful clarification, that the reconciliation of verse 20 includes "specially the intelligent universe"— people.[9] This is supported by the emphasis of verses 21–23 on reconciliation for the Colossian believers—and for you!

Therefore, the resultant "peace through the blood of his cross" (v. 20) applies not only to God's physical universe but also to His "intelligent universe." Compare Romans 5:1, "Therefore being justified by faith, we have peace with God through our Lord Jesus Christ." When you trust Christ as your Savior, what a glorious result! Look again at verse 20: He has made *peace,* through the blood of His cross.

S. Lewis Johnson asks: "In what sense can heaven itself be the object of Christ's reconciling work? . . . The answer to the problem is probably to be found in Paul's words in Romans 8:18–23. . . . The reconciling work of the Son of God, the representative Mediator, is destined to restore the whole creation to its determined order. When man's redemption according to the divine program for the ages is completed, then that redemption shall be extended to the entire physical creation."[10]

It is great to have peace with the law, isn't it? A few years ago in a Bible conference I used obedience to the law as an illustration of our love and obedience to the Lord.

Two years later we drove to the same conference, and I noticed a man following me for several miles in his car, but it seemed he did not want to pass me. I pulled into the conference center, and so did he. I went to register, and he parked and greeted me by saying, "Hello, Brother Gannett! Great to see you again," and then added, "I'm so glad you practice what you preach." He had followed me to see if I kept the law. It is wonderful to be at peace with the law—and it is infinitely better to be at peace with God's law.

Imputation (2 Cor. 5:19)

Turn for a moment to 2 Corinthians 5, where we discover two other glorious provisions of reconciliation. Verse 19 says, "God was in Christ, reconciling the world unto himself, not imputing their trespasses unto them." That means that when we trust His Son as our Savior, God no longer puts to our account our trespasses. They are no longer reckoned to the believer in time or eternity. Thank God!

Justification (2 Cor. 5:21)

Then there's a positive provision in verse 21. "For he hath made him to be sin for us, who knew no sin; that we might be made the righteousness of God in him." My standing and yours before God does not depend on how we live today or how we serve today. Our standing before God depends on the righteousness of God in Christ.

Presentation (1:21–22)

Our text in Colossians 1 sets out a fourth glorious provision. *"And you, that were sometimes alienated and enemies in your mind by wicked works, yet now hath he reconciled in the body of his flesh through death, to present you holy and unblamable and unreprovable in his sight."*

This speaks of that future day, the rapture of the church, when we will be caught up to be with the Lord. There our Bridegroom, the Lord Jesus Christ, will present us, His bride, to His Father. At the moment we are caught up, we will become totally like our Lord, morally and spiritually.

I shall never forget the first time I presented my bride-to-be to my parents. I had met her at Houghton College, a Christian school, and fell in love with her. I kept writing letters home about her. We wrote in those days.

Donald Grey Barnhouse was preaching in Rochester, New York, so my parents came over from our hometown, Geneva, New York, to meet my sweetheart. We came up from Houghton. Of course, we were late to the service, because we had already learned that the longest way around was the sweetest way.

After the service, we got together—mother and father, my bride-to-be and I. Soon my father had to go for the car that wintry February night, and my sweetheart had to go powder her nose, and that left Mother and me alone. Mother approvingly reported, "Son, your father said, 'Go to it!'"

Father knows best, I have heard. And some fifty years later I thank God with all my heart.

This is the moment of presentation in Colossians, only it will be the actual presentation. We will have been raptured, caught away. The dead in Christ will have been raised first, and then we will be caught up into the presence of our risen Lord, and there He will present us, His bride, to God His Father.

Paul concludes the paragraph by saying this presentation will occur for his readers (and for you and me) *"if ye continue in the faith grounded and settled, and be not moved away from the hope of the gospel, which ye have heard, and which was preached to every creature which is under heaven; whereof I Paul am made a minister"* (v. 23).

Paul did not say, "If you hang on, you'll get to heaven. If you work hard enough and live a good enough life, you'll make it to heaven." No, he said that your continuing in the faith is evidence that you are trusting Jesus Christ to be your Savior.

After an evening school class in Dallas, Texas, years ago, a businessman said to me, "Alden, I want you to have lunch with me," and we arranged a time. Upon my arrival, he closed the office door before we went to lunch and said, "I have a very important personal question to ask you. I made a profession of faith in Christ when I was seven years old, but I haven't lived it from that day to this, and I know it. Tell me: Am I a Christian?"

My heart responded immediately, *Probably not.* And I told him so. But I said, "In the final analysis, I am no one's judge. Do you believe the Bible to be the Word of God?" He answered, "Yes, sir, I do." "Do you believe Jesus Christ is the Son of God?" "Yes, sir, I do." "That He died on the cross for your sins and rose again?" "Indeed I do." As we bowed together across his desk, I said, "Mr. Jones [and that really was his name], I ask you now, in the presence of God, to pray these words after me." This was our prayer:

Father in heaven, I am not sure I was saved when I was a child. The evidence is not there. But now with all my heart I confess Jesus Christ to be the Son of God. I confess that He died on the cross for my sins and rose again. And Father, if I didn't do it sincerely before, now I trust Jesus Christ and Him alone to be my Savior.

He prayed that prayer sincerely, to make sure, and God saved him.

Dear reader, if you need to pray that prayer, pray it from your heart—now. And if you just did, the Bible says that you too are saved (Rom. 10:13).

The Communication of Christ (1:24–2:3)

After Paul's classic presentation of the doctrines of the person and work of Christ and prior to his exposure and correction of the error of the day—what we call the Colossian heresy—he feels constrained to linger a bit longer with his readers in regard to the important matter of his communication of Christ to others.

Observe first Paul's strategy of presenting truth before correcting error. Like the experienced bank teller with new employees, his approach is to acquaint his readers with the true currency, so to speak, so that when false currency passes through their hands, they will recognize it immediately. One cannot detect error until one first knows the truth.

Excited about the glorious truths he has written, Paul now must pause to emphasize his communication of truth to others. This he does in the following paragraph (1:23–2:3).

Here Paul further prepares his readers for dealing with the error at hand, the false teaching at Colosse. He does so by means of three great principles that will prove helpful in his communicating Christ to others: a twofold ministry; a twofold message; and a twofold method.

A twofold ministry (1:23–25)

To the unsaved (1:23)

Paul concludes verse 23, "[of which gospel] I Paul am made a minister." The great apostle wrote later to Pastor Timothy (2 Tim. 4:5), "Do the work of an evangelist." He set the example himself. He first went to the unsaved and along with others communicated the gospel "to every creature which is under heaven."

Homer A. Kent pauses to call Paul's language "a legitimate use of literary hyperbole . . . a generalization not requiring statistical exactness."[11] To Paul it was the "whosoever believeth gospel." It recognized no boundaries, whether racial, national, or regional. In obedience to our Lord's command (Mark 16:15), it had reached Rome, from which he was writing this letter, and had, according to William Hendriksen, "actually invaded every large center of the then known world."[12]

Paul rightly called himself a minister of the gospel. This was his first ministry.

And we must follow in his train. With all our Bible teaching in the church—and thank God for it—let us join with Paul in becoming "ambassadors for Christ," first pleading with the lost to be reconciled to God. We can do no better than to imitate him in his ministry.

To the church (1:24–25)

Paul now adds in verses 24 and 25 his second ministry—to the church.

"[I] *now rejoice in my sufferings for you* [a paradox], *and fill up that which is behind* [lacking] *of the afflictions of Christ in my flesh for his body's sake, which is the church: Whereof I am made a minister, according to the dispensation* [stewardship] *of God which is given to me for you, to fulfil* [complete] *the word of God."* Paul was first a minister to the unsaved, but also he was a minister to the church.

I am persuaded that the devil has gained a tremendous victory because God's people do not have Paul's biblically balanced ministry. I have discovered that it is hard to be biblically balanced.

On one occasion I was invited to a church in Birmingham, Alabama. As I often do, I said to the pastor, "How do you close your service?" (As you know, pastors have different ways of doing things.) He said, "We always give an invitation. *We are after souls!"* I got the message. Thank God for a pastor who is after souls. I am from the Bible belt, where so many of our evangelical churches preach the gospel Sunday morning, Sunday night, and Wednesday night and have two revivals a year when they bring in an evangelist to preach primarily the gospel for eight nights.

Then I find in another church the pastor teaches through one book, then through another book, but the church does not grow numerically. Very few people are being saved, and it does not seem to be a concern of the pastor.

Regularly I ask, "Pastor, how are things progressing in your church?" Too often his reply is "Well, so-so." I hear that often. Teaching, teaching, teaching. Thank God for faithful Bible teaching, but not at the expense of evangelism, of outreach, of a burden to see people saved. You cannot teach an unconverted man the deep things of God.

In this context of evangelism and edification, one of my successors at Southeastern Bible College, C. Sumner Wemp, shouted, "Marry the two. Marry evangelism with Bible teaching." Amen! That is the Book. It is in the Great Commission in Matthew 28:19–20. The text says literally, "Having gone, make disciples of all nations, by baptizing, by teaching," not just by going and evangelizing but also by teaching new converts to observe everything the Lord has commanded. You see? Both are in the Book and here in Colossians.

The church at Antioch not only shared the gospel, with the result that people were being saved. But they then brought in Barnabas, who led many more to Christ. Then they brought in Saul of Tarsus (later called Paul), and he taught the new converts for a whole year. So we see that the church has a twofold ministry.

Do you have that burden as an individual? Is your church characterized by this twofold ministry? Do you have an outreach that is effective so that your church is growing spiritually and numerically? If not, repent and pray that by God's grace both pastor and people will evangelize the lost and edify the church, the body of Christ. Again, the biblical plan is a twofold ministry.

When we took our babies home from the hospital, we understood that our new babies had to be fed, loved, and nurtured. Then we found that when they grew up and had our grandchildren, we started all over again. So, in the spiritual realm, the good Lord intends that we never stop evangelizing (bringing souls to new birth) and edifying (seeing them grow)— a twofold ministry.

A twofold message (1:26–27)

To the unsaved (1:19–23)

Paul's first message is for those of you who are unsaved. "Christ died for you." If you are not a Christian, this is what you need to hear, that "God so loved the world [you], that he gave his only begotten Son, that whosoever believeth in him should not perish, but have everlasting life" (John 3:16).

When Paul went to a mission field, the city of Corinth, he reported that he preached to them the gospel; they received the gospel; they stood by the gospel; and they were saved by the gospel (1 Cor.15:1–2).

What a spiritually dead person needs is spiritual life. What a sinner needs is the Savior. Sinners need to hear about Christ, to learn how wonderful He is, and to know that He is the Son of God. He did come to planet Earth in God's own time. He took on human flesh and died for our sins. Then He proved it all by His resurrection from the dead. That is what a sinner needs to know. Paul preached Christ and Him crucified.

So our message to the lost is Jesus Christ, the One who will give a dead person life, forgive sinners and make them children of God, make them fit for heaven, and then give grace to live holy lives and be righteous and godly in this present age. Sinners need to hear about Christ.

To the church (1:26–27)

What do churchgoers need? Here is God's message for the church: *"Even the mystery which hath been hidden from ages and from generations, but now is made manifest to his saints"* (v. 26).

God's message for the church is a mystery. And what is a mystery? Paul has defined it here. It is something hidden in previous ages but now made manifest. Another has called it "something heretofore concealed but now revealed." Paul says it is the message regarding Christ for the Christian. The mystery in Colossians 1:27 is that the Christ who died for us is *in* us. Paul says, *"To whom God would make known what is the riches* [the wealth] *of the glory of this mystery among the Gentiles."*

Robert L. Saucy says, "This mystery is amplified in the Ephesian epistle, where it is revealed that 'the Gentiles are fellow heirs, and fellow members of the body, and fellow partakers of the promise in Christ Jesus through the gospel.'"[13]

Paul's readers were primarily Gentiles, and he was the apostle to the Gentiles. The mystery is *"Christ in you* [Gentiles], *the hope of glory"*—that is, divine revelation of the indwelling Christ,[14] the earnest, so to speak, of the coming glory when we will be with Him and like Him forever and ever.

So the message to the unsaved person is that Christ died for you. The message to the saved, the believer, is that Christ lives in you. The message is still Christ. The emphasis is still Christ.

Paul puts it this way in Galatians 2:20, "I am crucified with Christ: nevertheless I live; yet not I, but Christ liveth [where?] in me: and the life which I now live in the flesh I live by the faith of [by faith in] the Son of God, who loved me, and gave himself for me."

When we live by faith in Christ, says Paul, Christ lives *in* us, through our personalities. He is regulating our minds, our thought processes through the course of the day; regulating our emotions, what we love and what we hate; regulating our wills when decisions are made all through the day, how to spend our time, energy, money, and so on. Christ living within regulates and controls the personality. And through these personalities overflow divine love, joy, peace, longsuffering, gentleness, goodness, faith, meekness, self-control. Christ lives *in me,* wrote Paul. It means to dwell thoroughly, dwell at home, to be perfectly at home in our hearts.

Again, it is by faith. Christ is already there if we are Christians. He came the moment we trusted Christ to be our Savior. But He does not live through our personalities until we let Him, until we trust Him to do so.

When Paul wrote to the Philippians, he stated it concisely: "For to me to live is Christ" (Phil. 1:21). Let us take that literally. "For to me to live is Christ, and to die is gain." Christian living is Christ living in us.

Paul writes in this letter to the Colossians, "When Christ, who is our life, shall appear, then shall ye also appear with him in glory" (3:4). Christ our Savior is to become our Lord, our very life.

This is not something mystical. This is a normal relationship with a person throughout the entire day, from our waking moment until the moment we retire. "Not I, but Christ liveth in me."

Do you understand this glorious truth? My opinion is that most Christians do not. Christian living is doing one's best, they think; it is trying harder, they affirm; it is living by the Ten Commandments and the Golden Rule.

It is not going to church and Sunday school, and putting our money in the offering plate, and doing our best during the week. All this is in the energy of the flesh. To the contrary, Christian living is supernatural. It is divine. It is Christ who energizes us and lives His perfect life through us as we trust Him to do so.

I grieve to say that in many circles, the church is characterized by legalism. And legalism, according to C. C. Ryrie, is defined as "a fleshly attitude which conforms to a code for the purpose of exalting self."[15] Grace is what Christ does; it is His favor to the undeserving. He gives us the wisdom, the power, the strength we need. The Second Person of the Godhead provides it moment by moment as we trust Him, one step at a time.

Paul meant what he said in Romans 6:14, "Ye are not under law, but under grace." We are saved by grace, and we live by grace. The Christ who died *for us* now lives *in us*. That is the message.

A twofold method (1:28–2:3)

Finally, there is a twofold method for communicating this message: *"Whom we preach,"* wrote Paul, not "what" (v. 28). Not the local newspaper, not *Time,* not the latest news on television, but "whom we preach." It is the Lord Jesus Christ, the One whom Paul has been talking about in the context.

Warning by the Word (1:28–29)

How did Paul proclaim Christ? First, by *"warning every man."* We parents have the responsibility of warning our children. If a boy chases another boy around the house with a knife in his hand, he needs to be warned.

When false teaching comes into the homes of our people, they need to be warned. When preaching, teaching, radio, television, or literature is contrary to the Word of God, people need to be warned. A faithful shepherd (Acts 20) warns. The apostle Paul warned the Ephesian elders. We proclaim Christ by warning people by means of the Word.

We proclaim Christ by *"teaching every man in all wisdom, that we may present every man* [every believer] *perfect* [fullgrown, mature] *in Christ Jesus."*

"Whereunto I also labor." I work at it! says Paul. *"Striving according to his* [God's] *working* [all of grace, all of God], *which worketh in me mightily."* He is saying, "The power of the risen Christ is within, and as we minister the Word of God, God is pleased to bless His Word and work as we minister that Word on a one-to-one basis." In Sunday school, or in a church, or in a Bible conference, we proclaim the Word.

"Why are you so emphatic about the Word, Paul?" That is what God has promised to bless. As he wrote in 2 Timothy 3:16–17, "All scripture is given by inspiration of God, and is profitable for doctrine, for reproof, for correction, for instruction in righteousness: that the man of God may be perfect, thoroughly furnished unto all good works."

God blesses His Word. People are convicted of sin by the Spirit through the Word. They are born again by the Word of God. They are cleansed by the Word, sanctified by the Word, guided by the Word. Every spiritual work is done by the Holy Spirit through the Word. No wonder the cults and the religious crowd do not emphasize the teaching of the Word of God—for that is what God blesses and uses.

So we proclaim Christ by means of the Word, by warning, by teaching everyone, to present every believer full-grown in Christ Jesus. Mom and Dad, I have just dumped a big task on your shoulders. God wants you to present your children someday before the Father full-grown in Christ.

Sunday school teachers, thank God if you had one more than last week, or five or ten more in your class than a year ago. But God wants something else. He wants every member of your class, when the Lord comes, to be presented full-grown in Christ.

Pastor, if you have missed it, this is a big responsibility for you. Have you been looking for something to do? Pastors do not look for something to do! You claim the grace of God for the time and energy and wisdom to do what has to be done.

I was a pastor long enough to know that a pastor never goes to bed at night with everything completed and behind him. There is always another book to read. Always, more preparation for the messages is needed. Always, there is somebody we should have visited.

God wants everyone in your assembly, everyone in your church presented full-grown in Christ Jesus! So you will be busy until the rapture, and I will be busy until the rapture, reaching out to souls to see them saved, reaching out to God's people, ministering to them, to present them full-grown in Christ Jesus.

The first method is the Word, always the Word!

Power through prayer (2:1–3)

The second method for communicating Christ to others is prayer. *"I would that ye knew what great conflict I have* [what great agony, in the original language] *for you, and for them at Laodicea, and for as many as have not seen my face in the flesh."*

From this text we conclude that Paul had never seen his readers, but he writes to them after the report of Epaphras, who came from Colosse to Rome.

What is Paul's prayer for his readers? First, a general statement: *"That their hearts might be comforted* [encouraged]" (v. 2). Everyone needs encouragement every day. We all have burdens. We all have problems. We all have needs. We welcome encouragement from the promises of God, from the character and integrity of God, the fact that God has promised to be faithful to His Word. A word in season. Encouragement.

While we were on the road eleven weeks one summer, we met a number of God's people who needed encouragement. One was a dear friend who booted me, humanly speaking, into the ministry when I was a teenager. Now both he and his wife are in very poor physical condition in their retirement years. Both need encouragement.

Thus we find that pastors, elders, deacons, Sunday school teachers all need encouragement. Paul, having emphasized the Word, prays that the Word of the Lord would bring encouragement to God's people.

Specifically, what does that encouragement include? *"Being knit together in love."* God's people are vital and exciting Christians when we love. Things are drab at home and at church when God's people do not love. But the fruit of the Spirit is— what? Love! The new commandment is to love one another as Christ loved us. We pray to be filled with that love.

Do we want a vital church family with the blessing of God? Then we are to be Spirit-filled Christians overflowing with divine love. We are to begin the day looking for someone to love, someone to encourage, someone to whom we can minister our wonderful Lord. Paul prays that love will so fill our lives—to what end? *"Unto all riches* [the wealth] *of the full assurance of understanding."* He prays for assurance, for the understanding of God's truth.

When a person doubts or questions, he or she is saying, "I really don't expect God to answer my prayer"; that person is not believing God's promises. He or she does not have conviction about the integrity of the promises of God.

So as believers in Christ, Christians need not only blessed assurance concerning their salvation; they also need that full assurance of God's truth of how to walk in the Spirit, how to pray, and to believe His glorious promises.

When this is the case, the result, verses 2 and 3 go on to say, will be *"the acknowledgment* [or full knowledge—experiential knowledge is the term] *of the mystery of God, and of the Father, and of Christ in whom are hid all the treasures of wisdom and knowledge."*

Then this experiential knowledge of the truth becomes ours. Not only do we learn that the Christ who died for us lives within us, but also Paul is praying that the knowledge will become ours in experience. Paul is praying that his readers will by the grace of God appropriate the life of the risen Christ, will appropriate His wisdom, His comfort, His encouragement, His grace, His strength, His power—whatever we need at the moment. Christ then becomes the truth that we need.

When this prayer is answered, I will in fact trust God. I will say, "I can do all things through Christ" (Phil. 4:13). I will claim the wisdom I lack at the moment for God to lead and give direction for whatever issues are at hand. This experiential knowledge, then, becomes mine.

The Word and prayer—these two principles are sufficient for communicating Christ through the apostle Paul, through you, and through me.

The Holy Spirit through Paul has reminded us that there is an unsaved world and that the message everyone needs is Christ. There is the church, the body of Christ, that needs revival and growth toward maturity in Christ. The message to those believers is the indwelling Christ. Our preeminent Christ is indeed all-sufficient.

Isn't it glorious to be a Christian and to have such provision every single day—this ministry of Christ through us!

Sinner and saint alike need every moment of every day the encouragement of the riches of grace in Christ Jesus our Lord.

It is no wonder Paul said we can do all things through Christ, who strengthens us. A few years ago my wife and I went to a hospital in Birmingham to visit a woman who was dying of cancer. As we walked into the room, her husband, a Gideon, thrust his Gideon New Testament into my hand and said, "Go talk to that woman," pointing to his wife's roommate. He was quite direct. I understood him well, so I took his Testament and walked around to the bedside.

I quickly learned that the woman was a Christian and that she was a member of a gospel-preaching church in the city. She attended Sunday school, church, and prayer meeting faithfully. She loved the Lord, His people, and His Word.

Three weeks earlier, she had learned that her daughter had left her husband and had gone to California, met another man, had immoral relations with him, conceived a baby, and then had an abortion. She phoned her mother to tell her what had happened.

The mother went to pieces. She became not only emotionally ill but also physically ill—so ill that the doctor put her in the hospital. She quit going to Sunday school and church, quit reading her Bible and praying, quit trusting the promises of God, and worried herself sick into the hospital. Isn't that a costly act of disobedience to God?

So I opened the Testament and began to quote and to read the Word, the glorious promise in the Old Testament: "Call unto me and I will answer thee, and shew thee great and mighty things, which thou knowest not" (Jer. 33:3), and some great promises of the New Testament, such as, "Ask, and it shall be given you; seek, and ye shall find; knock, and it shall be opened unto you" (Matt. 7:7). I reminded her that Jesus also said, "According to your faith be it unto you" (Matt. 9:29). I read psalm after psalm, promise after promise in the Scriptures.

Her tears began to dry. The joy of the Lord began to return to her countenance. I took her hand. I prayed with that brokenhearted mother, thanked God for who He is, thanked God that His promises are yea and amen, thanked God that His mercies are new every morning and great is His faithfulness. We thanked God that the Lord is our Shepherd and that we shall not want.

We continued in prayer together, rejoicing in the Lord, thanking Him for what we did not understand. We claimed His grace and wisdom and faithfulness and the grace to love that daughter and to welcome her home. We trusted Him to restore her to fellowship and to see the grace of God through the Word, and prayer begin to work in her life and restore her home.

When I left that bedside, that mother was rejoicing because of the grace of God and the promises of God.

I tell you, Christ in the life works, when He is all in all, *preeminent.* All this comes about when we have a vital, personal relationship with Christ, first as our Savior, then with Christ as our Lord and our very life.

Before we continue, pause a moment to review with me what God has said in His Word we are to do. If the reminder of the gospel is what you need, then lift your heart in faith to Jesus Christ, God's Son. Tell Him you believe He died on the cross for you and that you believe He was raised again the third day. With all your heart trust Jesus Christ to save you. Will you do that?

If you do not know that your sins are forgiven, that you have life in Christ, if you do not know the blessing and joy of being a Christian, but you want to be saved, cry out, "Lord, save me. I believe You are the Son of God. I believe You died for me. I now trust You and You alone to be my Savior." Pray that *now* from your heart.

If you prayed that prayer and trusted Christ as your Savior, give your pastor or a friend the privilege of leading you to the assurance of your salvation through the Scriptures. Let someone help you get started in living the Christian life.

My fellow Christian, let me encourage you to start now that life of faith, if you have not been living the Christian life. One step at a time, trust the Lord for grace for the need of the moment, claiming His grace for whatever the need may be. Trust Him for His grace to lead you and to enable you to live and serve for His glory.

Father, thank You for this time together around Your Son, through Your Word. Minister Your great grace to each of us in our growth in grace and knowledge of our wonderful Lord. We pray this through Jesus Christ Your Son. Amen.

THE COLOSSIAN HERESY
(2:4–3:4)

Notice the apostle's approach to the problem of false teaching. He does not minimize it, nor does he circumvent it. Rather, he names it forthrightly, explicitly defines it, and then helpfully corrects it with the true teaching found in Christ (that is, humanism is not according to Christ, v. 8).

At times we may have heard a lecture or a sermon on a controversial subject, and afterward we turned to the one beside us and asked, "What was his point? Where does he stand?" Not so with Paul. He is clear, candid, and loving in answering error directly with the truth.

We have watched the apostle Paul as he shared his personal greetings and expressed his thanksgiving to God for these Colossian believers and for the grace of God in them. Then he prayed for them that they might be filled with the Word. He has spoken to them about the person and work and ministry of our Lord Jesus Christ. That is how he has prepared his readers for what he now has to say about the false teaching, which he longs to refute in their thinking.

Paul continues the same preparation in Colossians 2:4–7. In verse 4 he writes, *"And this I say, lest any man should beguile you with enticing words."*

"Persuasive words" is the term. Isn't it amazing how eloquent many false teachers are? Be on the alert for that. So often liberal preachers are outstanding orators but deniers of Christ and deniers of the Word of God. They use persuasive words.

"For though I am absent in the flesh [Paul is in prison in Rome as he writes these words], *yet am I with you in spirit"* (v. 5). I pray for you, he says. My heart is with you as you are there countering the false teachers knocking on your door. I am *"joying and beholding your order* [a military term] *and the steadfastness of your faith in Christ."* From this verse I

conclude that the Colossian leaders had not succumbed to the false teaching of these heretics.

Paul further prepares his readers in verses 6 and 7 by writing, *"As ye have therefore received Christ Jesus the Lord, so walk ye in him: rooted and built up in him, and stablished in the faith, as ye have been taught, abounding with thanksgiving."*

Notice that Paul continues to speak of the Colossians' personal relationship with their Lord. He says, *"As ye have therefore received Christ Jesus the Lord, so walk ye in him."* He is saying simply, "You received Christ by faith; keep on living that way."

That should remind us, as I have said repeatedly, that the way we enter God's family is by receiving Christ Jesus the Lord by faith. John 1:12 says, "But as many as received him [a Person], to them gave he power to become the sons [children] of God, even to them that [do one thing] believe on his name." How do I receive Christ Jesus our Lord? John says by believing on His name.

In this letter to the Colossians, we have seen that Jesus Christ is the Son of God, our Creator, Sustainer, and Reconciler. He went to the cross of Calvary and made peace through the shedding of His blood. He is the One who died in our stead and bore our sins in His own body on the tree.

Paul says, "You at Colosse, I thank God that you have received Christ Jesus the Lord." In the light of this, "So walk ye in [union with] him." The tense says, Keep on walking in union with the risen Lord.

The apostle explains, "Rooted." The tense says that the roots, so to speak, go down into the grace of the risen Christ who lives within, and His grace keeps overflowing and more.

Paul then explains further, "[continually] built up in [union with] him." We keep growing in grace. We keep being built up in Christ, and thus he adds, "Established in the faith as ye have been taught." It is by the knowledge of this Book that we keep on growing in grace and in the knowledge of our Lord.

Finally, Paul adds, "abounding with thanksgiving." We offer thanksgiving for having received Christ Jesus the Lord, thanksgiving that we are in Christ, thanksgiving that we are rooted and continually built up in Him.

Paul's thanksgiving is all Christ-centered. All this truth is wrapped up in the person and work of our Lord Jesus Christ, who is central to everything in our Christian lives.

With this further preparation, Paul now faces head-on four errors of these Gnostics, so called because they claimed to teach superior knowledge, superior to what Epaphras, having been tutored by the apostle Paul, had taught at Colosse.

Philosophy (2:8–10)

The first error Paul calls "philosophy" in verse 8. Let us call it humanism because that is the label we give it today. He says, *"Beware lest any man spoil you* [that is, make a spoil of you, make you a prey, a captive] *through philosophy* [humanism] *and vain deceit, after the tradition of men, after the rudiments of the world, and not after Christ."*

Paul is not saying that philosophy, the love of wisdom, is sinful. It is this kind of philosophy that is sinful. He describes it as vain deceit, contrary to the Word of the living God. The false teachers insisted that the great purpose of life does not come from God's written Word.

This philosophy is not God's revelation at all. It is "the tradition of men." It is what our church has always taught us, what we have always believed, rather than what God's Word says. Paul says this philosophy is after the rudiments (the ABCs) of this sinful world.

If you were to be graduated from an outstanding university with a Ph.D. in philosophy, you would be considered in the academic world to be an outstanding intellectual, a keen mind indeed.

But if you were not a Christian and you studied this humanism, whose philosophy was agnostic and atheistic, God's commentary would be that what you have learned is kindergarten stuff. It is only human wisdom, just what depraved, sinful people have thought (again rudiments, the ABCs), rather than the truth, which is what God has written in His eternal Word.

What is wrong with that philosophy? Paul answers in the closing words of verse 8: it is simply "not after Christ." There is

God's yardstick. That is how He evaluates human wisdom. He says that humanism is not according to Christ.

In verse 3 of this chapter, Paul declared that in Christ are hidden all the treasures of wisdom and knowledge. So when human wisdom is contrary to God's written Word, it is error, because it is not according to Him who is the way, the truth, and the life. Our Lord prayed in John 17:17, "Sanctify them through thy truth: thy word is truth."

And so we evaluate everything by God's written Word. It is not truth because an outstanding scholar has written it or taught it. It is not truth because that scholar is a professor in a famous university with a prestigious name or that he is an outstanding scholar in his field. The criterion is, Does what is taught line up with God's eternal Word?

We are living in a day when most of our public schools and universities are riddled with humanism. Then we wonder why our generation is no longer interested in the Bible, in God and the things of God, in Jesus Christ His Son, and His eternal Word. We have done our best to train our children in our homes and in the church, but then we send them to liberal schools and wonder why so many of them are graduated as humanists.

I have been a Christian educator for more than forty years and have an M.A. from New York University in higher education. I sat there myself—educated by humanists. Nevertheless, thank God, there are some Christians on such faculties.

So I believe in *Christian* education from the cradle to the grave. I believe in training young people in the Word of God, as Deuteronomy 6 teaches. I know of nothing in my Bible that emphasizes that a Christian should become immersed in the wisdom of this world. The Old Testament prophets were commanded not to use even the name of another god. And in our liberal schools we have courses, if you please, on other gods. We do—humanism.

I warn you, from the Word of the Lord, against the wisdom and the teaching of our day. I am from the Bible belt (Birmingham, Alabama) now riddled with humanism. When we witness, we can no longer assume that people believe the Bible, believe in God, believe in Christ. Humanism has carried the day in our secular universities. (Thank God for the few exceptions.) Only God knows the destruction that has come from it. Again, what's wrong with it? It is not according to Christ.

In verses 9 and 10, Paul explains further, *"For in him* [Christ] *dwelleth all the fulness of the Godhead bodily."* Christ is bodily at the right hand of the Father, and in Him dwells all the fullness of God. "Deity [the divine attributes and nature] dwelt in His earthly body" as well.[1] *"And ye are complete* [filled full] *in him, which is the head of all principality and power."* Observe that according to Paul, our sphere of completeness is found only in Christ; thus "in union with Christ our every spiritual need is fully met. Possessing Him, we possess all. . . . He is 'the head,' in the sense that He is the source of life for all that exists and sovereign Lord over it all."[2]

Since we have the all-sufficient Savior, we do not need human wisdom. We do not need to live on the husks of the world's wisdom when we have the infinite wisdom of God written down for us in our language in His Book. We are complete—complete in Him.

Are you totally satisfied with Christ and with His infinite wisdom? What a glorious privilege indeed to know Him "in whom are hid all the treasures of wisdom and knowledge" (2:3).

Legalism (2:11–17)

The fact of new life in Christ (2:11–12)

The Judaizers' second error was a Jewish legalism. They did not teach *"circumcision made without hands, in putting off the body of the sins of the flesh by the circumcision of Christ"* (v. 11).

Robert G. Gromacki explains: "Inner, spiritual circumcision results 'in putting off the body of the sins of the flesh' ['the sins of' omitted in the Greek text]. This action occurs at conversion and removes the guilt, penalty, and pollution of the sin principle with its impure thoughts and deeds. It does not eradicate the sin nature, but it does strip away the power of the sin nature so that a believer does not need to obey its dictates anymore.

"This 'spiritual circumcision' is made possible . . . at the time of the conversion of the sinner when [Christ] applies the benefits of His death and resurrection."[3]

Paul is saying that when Christ died, He died to deal with our specific sins (plural); He died to deal with our sin nature, the flesh (singular), a truth Romans 6 emphasizes so strongly.

In verse 12 we read, *"Buried with him in baptism."* This is not water baptism, because public confession of faith is not the subject here. Rather, Paul is speaking of the baptizing of the Spirit, which unites believers to Christ and creates the church, the body of Christ (Rom. 6:3; 1 Cor. 12:12–13).

Verse 12 continues, *"Wherein also ye are risen with him through faith in the operation of God, who hath raised him from the dead."* Here is the glorious fact of new life in Christ, which those false teachers knew nothing about. Because we died with Christ, were buried with Him, and were raised in resurrection life and power with Him, we have the resurrection life of Jesus Christ within. We have life in Christ the Lord— divine life, spiritual life, and eternal life.

The features of new life in Christ (2:13–15)

Life itself (2:13a)

Paul describes the features of this new life in Christ (v. 13 and following), *"And you, being dead in your sins* [with reference to specific acts of sin] *and the uncircumcision of your flesh* [the old, carnal, selfish flesh, your sin nature] *hath he quickened* [made us alive] *together with him."* Note, Christ died with relation to both our specific sins and our sin nature.

The first feature of our new life in Christ in our text is life itself. We are alive in Jesus Christ our Lord. Ephesians 2 says we were dead in trespasses and sins, dead spiritually, and now that we have been saved by receiving Christ as our Savior, we have new life in Him—a life that loves the Lord, a life that loves holiness and righteousness, a life that loves the Word. We are now alive in Christ.

I shall never forget one Lord's Day afternoon in Birmingham when my wife and I went to a home where a loved one had died over the weekend. As we walked in, we greeted a woman we knew well from our evening school. She whispered to us, "Our niece is here, and I spent until midnight last night witnessing to her, but she is still not saved." She looked me straight in the eye, and I responded accordingly.

Once we were introduced to the niece, this woman and my wife lingered in the living room, and the niece and I went to the kitchen where we sat down at the table. In the context of a sleeping baby in her arms, I shared the wonderful gospel of our Savior with her.

I am delighted to say that after an hour or so she was ready to receive Christ. We bowed together and she called on the name of the Lord to save her. Then I prayed, and as soon as I said, "Amen," she said, "Oh! I want my husband to be saved too!" She had life. Her first utterance as a new Christian was "I want my husband to be saved too." This was an evidence of life.

Do you have life? Not a ritual, not empty formalism, but do you have life in Jesus Christ? The Colossians had new life because they received Christ Jesus the Lord. If you have never done so, do so now.

Forgiveness (2:13b)

The second feature of this new life (v. 13b) is that God has *"forgiven you all trespasses."* Isn't that glorious! Is there any one of us who wants to confess all our trespasses publicly? Not one of us. Thank the Lord, we do not have to. The moment we trusted Christ as Savior, says Paul, God in heaven forgave all our past, present, and future sins.

In terms of our standing in the courts of heaven, my fellow Christian, we have been forgiven *all* trespasses. Not one sin is held against us. We have been forgiven all.

Freedom from the law (2:14)

The third feature of this new life is the *"blotting out the handwriting of ordinances that was against us."* What is the handwriting? It was the Ten Commandments, written by the finger of God, the two tablets of stone at Sinai. Paul rejoices that God has blotted out the handwriting of ordinances that was against us. The children of Israel had said, "All that the Lord hath spoken we will do" (Ex. 19:8). But they did not obey.

Paul goes on to say that the handwriting of ordinances *"was contrary to us."* Here was the demand to do right—but without the enabling grace to do right, to obey God's Word.

It was contrary to us, but God in Christ *"took it out of the way, nailing it to his cross."* Free from the Law! Oh, happy condition! Paul shouts and we sing, and rightly so, because Paul wrote to the Romans, "Ye are not under the law, but under grace" (6:14).

Deliverance from evil powers (2:15)

Paul adds further in verse 15, *"having spoiled [put off] principalities and powers."* This refers to Satan and his hosts. God "made a public spectacle of them, triumphing over them by the cross" (NIV).

When Jesus Christ died on the cross, He not only died for our sins and our sin nature but also died, as we read in Hebrews 2:14, to deliver us from the devil and his demons, having gained the victory through His death on the cross.

Here is deliverance from principalities and powers, accomplished by the death of our Lord Jesus Christ. Oh, how great it is to know the Savior who died for us and provided such glorious release and victory.

Now Paul makes his own application in verses 16 and 17. *"Let no man therefore judge you in food, or in drink, or in respect of an holyday, or of the new moon, or of the sabbath days."* He is talking about Judaism, the ceremonial law that was dealt a death blow on the cross of Calvary.

Obviously from the context we conclude that Paul is delineating in verses 11 through 17 the false teaching of these so-called Gnostics at Colosse, and by contrast the riches of grace in Christ Jesus our Lord. These false teachers had not comprehended the new age of grace.

"The new age," says S. Lewis Johnson, "is not an extension of Judaism; rather Judaism was a mere shadow of the present age."[4]

Grace is revolutionary, Paul insists. It is what Thomas Chalmers eloquently called "the expulsive power of a new affection," the power of the risen Christ residing in the believer.

What these false teachers were expounding is contrary to the grace taught by Christ in Mark 7:15–19; to the grace visualized in Peter's vision of Acts 10; to the grace expounded throughout the epistles of Paul, particularly in Romans 6:14, "Ye are not under the law, but under grace."

Hence Paul's application in verses 16 and 17, "Let no man, therefore, judge you." The present tense of the imperative *(krineto)* indicates that the heretics and their converts constantly had been criticizing the lack of legal conformity in the church.

Paul insists that the false teachers are substituting mere shadows for the substance, for the reality, our Lord Jesus Christ—*grace.*

I proposed to my sweetheart the last night before we left college our first year. I wanted to get things nailed down before someone else stepped in. So I proposed to her, and she responded positively, thank God.

Well, June 21 was her birthday. We lived only 250 miles apart, and while that was a long distance in those days, I nevertheless had to be there to help celebrate her birthday in Oil City, Pennsylvania. I knocked on the door. She came down the steps, opened the door, and saw who was there. She closed the door, went back upstairs, picked up my picture, and kissed the picture. (You don't believe that, do you? Nor do I.)

I am simply saying, "Who wants the picture when the reality is here?" So many features of the Old Testament anticipated the coming of Christ, anticipated His death on the cross. They were just types, just shadows.

But now Christ has come. The reality is here. The Son of God Himself came down to planet Earth and died for our sins and rose again. We do not need the shadows, the pictures, anymore. The living Christ Himself has come. And we are "complete in him."

Mysticism (2:18–19)

Another area of false teaching reported by Epaphras to Paul in Rome is recorded in verses 18 and 19—Oriental mysticism. And what is that? you ask. Paul answers, *"Let no man beguile you of your reward in a voluntary humility and worshipping of angels, intruding into those things which he hath not* [the word *not* is omitted in the better manuscripts] *seen, vainly puffed up by his fleshly mind."*

Before Paul spells out the nature of mysticism, he gives a warning to the Colossian believers not to allow the false teachers to lead them astray with error and hence lose their approval before the Lord and the rewards He promises to the faithful.

We in the United States remember well the young woman who was honored as Miss America in 1983, only later to lose her reward because it was learned that she earlier had disqualified herself from entering the contest. So, the believers at Colosse are duly warned by Paul not to lose their reward by losing the approval of the Lord.

Mysticism embraced three areas of false teaching: a carnal humility, a carnal worship, and a carnal pride. The mystics' carnal humility was expressed by their false humility in their worship of angels, which, says Warren W. Wiersbe, is "the belief that a person can have an immediate experience with the spiritual world, completely apart from the Word of God and the Spirit of God."[5]

My father employed a number of Italians, dear people who taught me to love spaghetti. They would take me to their homes and would serve me my favorite food. One woman's name was Rose. She was such a devout Roman Catholic that she was in church every morning of the year at 5 o'clock to celebrate mass. How devoted she was to her faith.

I said to her one day, "Rose, tell me, why do you pray to Mary?" "Oh," she replied, "I am so sinful. Jesus Christ would never listen to me. But if I pray to Mary, she will share my requests with her son, Jesus. Jesus will hear my request and answer my prayer." This is somewhat analogous to worshiping angels. Paul urged the Colossians not to disqualify themselves before God through such a carnal humility, when the Bible invites believers to "come boldly unto the throne of grace, that we may obtain mercy, and find grace to help in time of need" (Heb. 4:16).

The second error of these mystics was a carnal worship, the professing of a higher spiritual experience through claiming to have had visions.

All that is contrary to Revelation 22:19, which says we are not to add to God's Word or to take away from God's Word. So there have been no added revelations from God since the first century of the church.

Some years ago, I was ministering in Independence, Missouri, the home of the late President Truman. My host pastor asked me if I would like to see the headquarters of the break from Mormonism. I said, "Surely." So we were given a tour of the facilities. We came to a certain spot, and our tour guide said, "Do you see that spot there on the floor?" We nodded, and she continued, "God gave me a vision right there. I was on my knees praying, and oh, God gave me such a glorious vision!"

There are no additions to God's eternal Word! Hence, what she called a vision was contrary to the Bible, and anything contrary to the Bible cannot be true. Amen.

What was the third basic problem of these mystics? We have seen that one problem was the worship of God's creatures—angels; the second was visions; now Paul adds a third error, humans being puffed up by their fleshly minds—carnal pride.

Paul summarized in verse 19. They were *"not holding the Head,"* that is, "did not elevate Christ." "The negative," Gromacki continues, "is very emphatic, and the present participle *(kraton)* shows that such were continually not elevating the Savior."[6] "The mystic does not cling to Christ. He fails to see that Christ is all-sufficient for salvation, and that all the treasures of wisdom and knowledge are hidden in Him (Colossians 2:3, 9, 10)."[7]

The failure of the mystics was their "not holding the Head." This failure is a violation of a proper relationship to Jesus Christ, that of abiding in Him (John 15:5).

Asceticism (2:20–3:4)

Beginning at verse 20, we read of one more false teaching—asceticism. That is the belief that matter is evil, the physical body is evil. Jesus Christ, ascetics insist, is not the God-Man, because He has a human body. So, they teach, God came upon Jesus at His baptism and departed from Jesus on the cross; according to them, Christ is not the Son of God.

Paul writes (vv. 20–23), *"Wherefore if* [better, since] *ye died with Christ, from the rudiments of the world* [the ABCs of the world], *why, as though living in the world, are ye subject to ordinances* [NASB "such as"], *touch not; taste not; handle not."*

If you have another version, the order is reversed, but the truth is there. Don't touch anything that is physical. Don't taste. Don't handle, *"which all are to perish with the using, after the commandments and doctrines of men."*

Paul continues in verse 23, *"Which things have indeed a show of wisdom in will worship, and humility, and neglecting of the body."* There it is—neglecting of the body because it is sinful, they insist. Paul continues, such is *"not in any honour* [better, of no value] *to the satisfying of* [or the victory over the sinful nature] *the flesh."* They think one becomes spiritual when he touches not, tastes not, and handles not.

Our Roman Catholic friends finally awakened to the fact that eating hamburgers on Friday is not sinful. Where in the world they ever got the idea that eating a hamburger is sinful and the eating of fish is spiritual, I do not know. I have read my Bible many times, and I have not found it yet. Finally they too discovered that it was not in the Bible. So Roman Catholics can now eat steak on Friday.

You see the principle? These Judaizers thought that what was physical was sinful. Notice, evaluates Paul, such are "after the commandments and doctrines of men" (v. 22). "These things have indeed a show of wisdom [hypocrisy] in will worship [originated within the human will], and humility, and neglecting of the body, not in any honor [value, above] to the satisfying of the flesh."

When I was in college, a dear brother was having a difficult time in his walk with God. He dearly loved the Lord. He was a man of God, and I would not make light of him for a moment. But he had some unusual ideas. He felt that he was out of fellowship with the Lord for some reason, and he testified, "I got up at 4:30 in the morning, and I was in my haymow crying out and praying and asking God to show me what my problem was. And the Holy Spirit showed me. Praise the Lord! He told me to take off my necktie. Now I have glorious victory. Hallelujah! Praise the Lord!" Tell me, in which book of the Bible does it tell you that a necktie is carnal?

On another occasion, I was with the Gideons in the Carolinas a few years ago over Labor Day, and a woman there told me about something that had recently happened in a church in her hometown. She said a man had just moved into the community, was looking for a church, and visited this particular one. He very much appreciated the Word, loved to hear the gospel proclaimed, and he said to the pastor as he went out the door, "I've enjoyed the service this morning greatly. We are new in town, and I'll be back tonight, the Lord willing." And the pastor said, "No, you will not, unless you shave off your beard this afternoon."

Where in the Bible does it tell us that wearing a beard is harmful and devilish? But we do have our tastes. God calls such "the commandments and doctrines of men."

Notice again Paul's response in Colossians 3:1, *"If* [since] *ye then be risen with Christ, seek those things which are above, where Christ sitteth on the right hand of God."* Who is above? Christ, sitting at the Father's right hand. Paul continues in verse 2, *"Set your affection* [mind] *on things above, not on things on the earth."* What is on the earth? Humanism, legalism, mysticism, and asceticism. All are human. All are of time and sense.

In verses 3 and 4, Paul explains, *"For ye are dead."* You died with Christ. You died to all of this. *"Your life is hid with Christ in God. When Christ, who is our life, shall appear, then shall ye also appear with him in glory."*

You died with Christ on the cross to all of this. Christ is seated at the Father's right hand. Christ is our life (v. 4). Not only our Savior, not only our Lord, He is life itself! That is what the Bible says. "Christ liveth in me," wrote Paul in Galatians 2:20.

Here, Christ is our life. And He says that in the future we are going to appear with Him in glory, and bask in His glory, and reflect His glory, and experience His glory all through the eternal ages. Christian living is not humanism. It is not legalism, mysticism, or asceticism. Christian living is Christ! And you, fellow Christian, "are complete in him" (2:10).

A Concluding Question (2:6–7)

How does this truth regarding Christ as my life become mine in experience? I have been hinting at it throughout these studies.

Let us go back to Colossians 2:6–7. "As ye have therefore received Christ Jesus the Lord [by faith], so walk ye in [union with] him."

I live the Christian life exactly the way I was saved. I was saved by faith. I live the Christian life by faith.

Have you noticed how frequently the Bible uses the term *walk*? It is everywhere in the Scriptures. "Walk in love." "Walk worthy of the Lord." "Walk in the light."

How does one walk? You don't remember how you learned to walk as a small child, but you do remember teaching your children and your grandchildren to walk. You recall how they walked around the coffee table. Remember how they grabbed your finger and strengthened their little legs?

Pretty soon little Johnny let go and fell and bawled and squalled. The next time he fell and bawled. But the next time he fell, he got up and took over the house. And all the lovely trinkets had to be put up in the cupboards, because little Johnny had learned something profound: to depend, to rely; he knew his legs could support and carry him. We have a theological word for that: faith. "The just shall live by his faith" (Hab. 2:4).

There is a principle I want you to remember about walking. Is standing walking? No, standing is not walking. Is sitting walking? No, sitting is not walking. Is jumping walking? No. But such is the experience a lot of people are seeking these days. According to the Bible, it is not a crisis experience we should be seeking. We are to seek the Lord (Isa. 55:6).

Second, walking is continually depending upon the Lord. In the process of walking, we keep on depending. We keep on relying upon the risen Lord within.

The third principle about walking (this took college, seminary, and graduate school, so it is profound)—walking is one step at a time.

That is life. One moment at a time. One minute at a time. One hour at a time. One day at a time. One temptation at a time. One opportunity to witness at a time. One opportunity to serve Christ at a time.

You see, each time the occasion arises through the day, one can say, "Lord, help me. Lord, I claim your grace. Lord, I reckon myself dead to that sin but alive unto God." Use whichever phrase you are comfortable with. Say it the way you prefer, but say it. "Lord, I trust You for grace for this. I claim Your grace for that. I can do all things through You." At that split second when you exercise faith, God gives you victory through Jesus Christ our Lord.

It is important to be saved and cleansed. It is important to dedicate your life totally to the Lord. Total commitment to Him, yes. But He does not stop there. Next we must walk in faith through the course of the day, for every moment of the day, by faith.

When temptation comes, or when the opportunity to serve comes, we are to cry, "Lord, help me." "Lord, help me." "Lord, help me." And He does. There is always glorious victory through Jesus Christ our Lord. That's New Testament Christian living, and we found it in the Book.

Father, with all our hearts we do thank You for the privilege of walking in union with our living Christ. Thank You for that infinite "grace" within us. With Paul we pray that we may know Him and the power of His resurrection. We thank You for your love, Father.

And now give us the grace, one step at a time, to appropriate faith and to make it ours. May our days ahead be triumphant days, victorious days, fruitful days, because one step at a time we walk and live in union with our risen Lord. For this bountiful provision, our Father, we thank You in the name of Christ, our Savior. Amen.

Chapter 4

PRACTICAL CHRISTIAN LIVING
(3:5–17)

We begin with Colossians 3:5, where the apostle Paul turns to what has been called the hortatory section of the letter. That is, Paul makes the truth of Christ in the life very practical, down where we live.

It is important, as we begin, to recognize the context in which these verses are placed. Otherwise, all I have for you is good advice, and you are not seeking that. The critical point Paul makes in this remaining part of his letter is that the key to down-to-earth, practical, victorious, fruitful Christian living is Christ in the life.

A further introductory word is in order before we turn to the details of this new lesson. Christian living is made up of specifics. Some people have the notion that Christian living is walking around about six inches off the floor, with hands in the air, shouting "Glory!" Not for one moment. We have seen in this epistle that Christian living is Christ. It is a Person living through these personalities of ours. And the outliving of this Person, Christ in the life, is expressed in specifics.

And let me warn you that specifics are not to be equated with legalism, as is done so often. Some people cry "legalism" at the mention of specifics, negative or positive. I remind you of Ryrie's definition of legalism: "a fleshly attitude which conforms to a code for the purpose of exalting self."

I therefore suggest that when certain vices are forbidden in Scripture, as here in Colossians, they are enumerated as a plea to live righteously. And when specific virtues are mentioned in the New Testament, they are set forth in the context of grace— virtues fulfilled by Christ living within.

We are going to be discussing such specifics as fornication, covetousness, anger, love, and mercy. When you bake a pie (and I know very little about baking a pie), you use certain ingredients.

If you make an apple pie, I do know it includes apples and some flour, and if I recall correctly, some sugar is added. I am lost from that point on. But you know very well that it takes specifics to make a pie. And it takes specifics, beautiful virtues, to make a godly life that is pleasing to the Lord and honoring to Him.

These specifics are both negative and positive—vices to put off and virtues to put on. There are vices, and they are not in keeping with the risen Christ within. They dishonor Him, displease Him, and grieve Him, as Paul tells us in Ephesians 4. However, there are beautiful virtues that we can put on by the grace of God, which truly honor the Lord, please Him, and make our Christian lives reflect the very character of our Lord Himself.

Vices to Be Put Off *(3:5–11)*

With that introduction, look with me now at Colossians 3:5–17. We find three imperatives. The first is, *"Mortify therefore your members which are upon the earth."* That word *mortify* is a strange expression. It is an unusual word in English.

When I read this verse, I am reminded of one of our students who offered to paint our living room in our home in Birmingham. We came home about 3 o'clock in the afternoon, and our painter was on the floor, scraping up a gallon of paint that had fallen off the ladder. He was mortified.

To better understand this difficult term, let me suggest the translation of the New American Standard Bible, "Therefore consider the members of your earthly body as dead," that is, deprive them of power—your tongue, your hands, your feet, your body. And now Paul becomes specific.

"Fornication." Every one of us has the potential of being guilty of this awful sin. So Paul cries, "Deprive your bodies of this sin of immorality." He exhorts that this victory can be yours and mine through Christ who lives within. We have the grace, the power to say no to that temptation and to flee this lust.

He adds, *"uncleanness,"* a broader word for impurity, a word that includes the perversions of our day, of men with men and

women with women. This too is sin, in case you have been mis-
led to think otherwise. The Bible is very clear. Romans 1 names
specific sins on which the judgment of God falls, and this is one
of them. Apparently the judgment of God has already begun to
fall, with the multiplying cases of AIDS. The apostle Paul encourages us that Christ in the life can keep us from the immorality and the perversions of the day in which we live.

Paul continues, *"inordinate affection"* or "uncontrollable desires." Whenever anyone or anything masters you and me, it is
taking the place of the lordship of Jesus Christ within. I think
one of the greatest masters of people, including multitudes of
us Christians, is television.

Yes, we have television at our house. But when television is
more important than my devotions, family worship, or my study
time, or when that tube has that which dishonors God and
man, it must not be aired in our home. Nor yours. When it
becomes my master, I must turn it off. Do I?

Golf can be our master as can tennis, fishing, cars, or clothes.
Is Jesus Christ Lord of your life? He can be, by the grace of
God, and will be when you trust Him to take control.

Paul now adds, *"evil desire."* We can have pure and holy
desires, of course. Here the emphasis is on evil desires. They
are to have no place in our lives. Anything that is wrong, anything that is evil, anything that does not glorify our God must
go, because it does not honor Him. We are to deprive of power
whatever evil desire is in our lives.

Next he mentions *"covetousness,"* which is idolatry. Young
people, I have an apology to make to you. We adults have raised
you in a generation in which things are too important. I grieve
to say that. Along with a sex-ridden age, we are living in a
materialistic age. Too many of us adults have not set the proper
example. We spend so much time in employment that we do
not have enough time for our families. We do not have adequate
time for spiritual activities. At times we are too busy making
another dollar. We have to pay bills at our house too, as you do.
It is not money that is the root of all evil. It is the *love* of money,
Paul wrote in 1 Timothy 6:10.

Job in the Old Testament was rich. So was Abraham. It is not sinful to be rich. The question is, How do I use the riches God has entrusted to me to glorify Him?

When money is my master, Paul says it is like going into a church (as so many do) and bowing before a graven image. There is no difference. I would not be caught dead bowing before a carved image, because according to the Book of Exodus I would be committing idolatry. But have I been guilty of covetousness? How wrong, how sinful, how dishonoring to my God. However, I can take what God has entrusted to me and use it to the glory of God and have it further the gospel, when Christ is Lord, when Christ is in control of my life.

Paul explains in verse 6. *"For which things' sake the wrath of God cometh on the children of disobedience: in the which ye also walked sometime, when ye lived in them."* Paul is also saying that this lifestyle characterizes unsaved people. These sins are to have no place in the Christian's life, once Christ has saved us, has come to dwell within, and has given us the grace to live holy and righteously and godly in this present age. Christ within has the grace to say No! Grace to flee! Grace to bow before our Lord and crown Him Lord of all.

The second imperative Paul uses is in verse 8. *"But now ye also put off all these."* The term *put off* is what some of us do before we go to church. We put off a dirty shirt and put on a clean one. Here are some dirty shirts that by the grace of God we are to put off.

The first one Paul names is *"anger."* (Now he's gone to meddlin'.) How in the world do we put it off? How do we control our tongue? Our temper? Our emotions? By Christ in the life.

Next on the list is *"wrath."* What is that? Anger having reached the boiling point when the lid blows off! Ever been there?

"Malice." This means how I am going to get even. I have lost my temper over a certain matter. I am as angry as I can be, and now I am wondering how I can get even, how I can handle things and work it out so that I can hurt the person with whom I am angry.

Some years ago (in the days before four-lane highways) I was teaching this chapter in a conference, and a big, burly truck driver came to me and said, "Preacher, I've got a problem. I'll be driving my semi and some woman will cut in front of me, and that just makes me boil!" (Why he picked on women I don't know.) "So I wait for a good, long, straight stretch of road," he continued, "and I'll pull up beside that woman and force her right off the road! And boy, then I feel so much better. Is there help for me?"

Yes, sir! The answer is Christ in the life. Christ in the life can control our emotions. Christ in the life can help a person gain self-control, by the grace of God.

Paul adds, *"blasphemy."* Slander. Do you slander people? Do you speak evil against them? Do you spread gossip when you do not know whether or not it is true? According to our text, it dishonors God and people. Are you guilty of that at all? Is there any hope for a person who does that? Yes, Christ in the life. For when He lives within, He can control what I think. He can control my tongue. He can control what I say when I trust Him to do so.

Next Paul adds, *"filthy communication out of your mouth."* Dr. H. A. Ironside in his book on Colossians tells about a preachers' meeting he attended. The ladies had departed to prepare the lunch, and so the men were left alone together. One of the brethren spoke up and said, "Now that the ladies have gone, I have a story for us." Then Dr. Ironside interrupted the story-teller and said, "Sir, it is true that the ladies are not present, but the Holy Spirit is present." That stopped the story. Christ can control language. He can control what comes out of our mouths, so that everything we say is edifying. By Christ within!

Paul's third imperative is listed in verse 9: *"Lie not one to another."* Is Paul suggesting that Christians lie? I know a mother who was concerned about her daughter. She and her husband were saying, "Oh, we wish our daughter would social-ize with the young people in the church." But instead she was making friends only with non-Christians.

The parents insisted, so the daughter worked things out so that her parents would give permission for her to go to one of the homes of the young people of the church. After meeting there first, they would go elsewhere and do the things they wanted to do. *"Lie not one to another."* The daughter ultimately realized, thank God, that she had not put off the old life with its deeds and therefore had acted that way.

The reason such practices as lying could not be permitted, as Paul goes on to explain, is that the Colossian believers had already *"put off the old man with his deeds"* and had *"put on the new man, which is renewed in knowledge after the image of him that had created him."*[1]

Renald E. Showers writes, "at the moment of regeneration the person becomes the new man with the new disposition [new nature] and the indwelling Holy Spirit. Although he is the new man with a new moral outlook, the regenerated person is not morally perfect as God is perfect. Because he still possesses the sinful disposition [the old nature], he continues to be susceptible to its evil influence. For this reason, he must go through a process of growth, being motivated by the new disposition and empowered by the Holy Spirit and winning one victory after another over the sinful disposition, until he is perfectly conformed to the image of God and Christ when he sees Christ."[2]

Warren W. Wiersbe summarizes the Christian's experience well. He says that the once-for-all actions of putting off and putting on lead the believer on from "the *crisis* of salvation" to "the *process* of sanctification," becoming more like Jesus Christ. He then adds, "Man, initially *formed* in the image of God, then *deformed* from God's image by sin, through Jesus Christ can be *transformed* as we grow in the knowledge of the Word of God (v. 10)."[3]

And Robert G. Gromacki adds, "The result is the spiritual oneness of every believer regardless of his race, religion, culture, or social status (v. 11). While in actual life these classifications remain, nevertheless in the church and in Christ they are erased."[4]

Isn't it great to be a Christian? According to Colossians 3:5–11, Jesus Christ can give us grace to put off all the vices we have just seen, all that dishonors our Lord and hurts the testimony of our Lord. With this, Paul has encouraged us. We have put off the old man at regeneration; we have put on the new man, which is being renewed day by day.

Virtues to Be Put On *(3:12–17)*

Now Paul turns the coin over, beginning with verse 12. To change the metaphor, he does not eat away the donut and leave us with the hole. Here are positive things to take the place of the vices, beautiful virtues that honor our wonderful Lord.

"Put on, therefore, as the elect of God, holy and beloved" (v. 12). What he is saying is, "Act now according to what you are, an elect one, holy, beloved of God." Instead of putting on a dirty shirt, so to speak, put on a clean shirt. Put on a beautiful dress.

"Put on bowels of mercies," that is, a heart of compassion, an attitude that does not just put up with people, but a heart that reaches out to people who are hurting and to those who are burdened. It is more than saying, "Well, I'll try to be a gentleman or a lady and try to behave myself." No, my heart responds to them, reaches out to them by the grace of God to help them, to meet their needs.

A heart of compassion. Does your heart so respond? Or do you go about your business? Some such people are lost and on their way to hell. Others hurt deeply. Some have lost loved ones. Others have lost their jobs. Still others are having a hard time trying to make ends meet financially. Do you reach out to them, or doesn't it matter?

We put on a heart of compassion by faith; then Christ in the life overflows with a heart for people as they are.

Then Paul adds, *"Put on ... kindness,"* sweet Christian kindness, not the sharp tongue or the cutting remarks, but rather that soft answer that turns away wrath. "It is kindness expressed in attitude and deed,"[5] says Fritz Rienecker. How do I get that beautiful grace? Christ in the life.

Next Paul exhorts, *"Put on ... humbleness of mind."* We do not come by that naturally, do we? We are all better than someone else. Somebody told me facetiously about a book called *The World's Ten Most Humble People and How I Chose the Other Nine.* Were you the author? How does one get humble? Wives have a wonderful ability to do that for their husbands! Christ in the life is the answer, the One who is meek and lowly in heart.

Paul now adds, *"meekness."* You may have a version that translates this "gentleness," a beautiful Christian virtue. It refers to that gentleness which accepts our lot when God has taken home a loved one. You have had a permanent injury; here is the grace to accept your lot. You are thirty-five years old and not married yet, but you would like to be. Your child was born with a serious deformity; here is the grace to accept your lot—marvelous grace. Where do we get this? Christ in the life.

"Longsuffering." We saw in Colossians 1 that God's power gives us grace to be patient and longsuffering. Longsuffering, you will remember, is steadfastness in the hour of oppression— when people oppress or malign you, when people speak evil of you. Here is the grace to reach out and suffer long, and even minister to such people. Where do you get that grace? Chapter 1 says, "Be filled with the Word." This chapter says that when you are filled with the Word, Christ is yours experientially, and you learn to appropriate His grace by faith.

Then we move to verse 13. *"Forbearing one another."* That means putting up with one another. Is anyone in your church hard to put up with? You might find that person if you look in your mirror.

I was ministering in New Jersey in a conference, where on Thursday of each week some of the local Christians have a luncheon. I was the invited guest on that particular Thursday. As soon as I walked in, a brother got up and smiled, took my hand, and gave me a warm welcome.

My host welcomed me to the speaker's table and said, "Do you know that fellow?" I said, "Yes, I have met him before." He said, "He is the trouble maker of the whole community. He joins one church and tears it up, joins another church and tears it up, and goes on to the third. In fact, the other day I was talking with the pastor of the church he joined last, and I said, 'How are things going, Pastor, with So-and-So as a new member?' The pastor replied, 'Oh, he is making a spiritual contribution to our ministry.' 'How is that?' I asked. The pastor said, 'He keeps us on our knees!'"

Some people we put up with, and by the grace of God we do it lovingly and kindly and graciously.

Then Paul adds, *"forgiving one another."* (He goes to meddlin' here, sure enough.) Numbers of times in the ministry, people have confided to us that they do not have the grace to forgive.

Not long ago I said to a neighbor, "Did you have a wonderful Christmas this year? Did you have all the family together for the holidays?" The answer was, "Everybody but one sister. We've never been able to forgive her for what she has done to us."

A woman in Birmingham came to our evening school faithfully on Monday nights. She said, "Brother Gannett, my sister and I have lived beside each other in two different houses for twenty years and we haven't set foot in each other's house once."

What is the answer to an unforgiving spirit? Paul goes on to tell us in verse 13, *"If any man have a quarrel against any; even as Christ forgave you, so also do ye."* Our Lord on the cross prayed for His murderers, "Father, forgive them; for they know not what they do" (Luke 23:34). If Christ can forgive murderers, Christ in the life through you and me can forgive the people who never repaid us the money they borrowed or who speak lies about us. Have you been willing to forgive? Christ in the life can give you that grace.

What about Stephen? As he was being murdered, he saw the Lord standing, and he prayed while the rocks were being thrown at him, "Lord, lay not this sin to their charge" (Acts 7:60). Yes, there is grace for forgiveness. And if we need any more illustrations, let us look in the mirror and realize how much the Lord has forgiven you and me. Then let us thank Him.

Paul adds in verse 14, *"Above all these things put on charity* [love], *which is the bond of perfectness."* Cement, if you please. Or those steel bands that hold barrel staves in place. The bond of completeness holds everything together. *"Above all* [because love is the most important moral quality in the believer's life]," Paul concludes, *"put on love."*[6]

How do we know when we have put off that which dishonors our Lord and when we have put on that which pleases Him? Let me say it again, Christ in the life.

Verses 15 and 16 provide two tests. The subjective test is within us, *"Let the peace of God* [Christ, the better manuscripts render] *rule in your hearts, to the which also ye are called in one body; and be ye thankful."* Paul says that is the question. Does the peace of Christ rule in your heart at any given moment regarding any given issue? Or do you have a doubt? Do you wonder?

You will remember that Paul wrote in Romans 14:23, "Whatsoever is not of faith is sin." If I do something and I am not sure it is right, not sure it pleases my Lord, but I go ahead and do it anyway, it is sin whether it was right or wrong, because I did it not in faith.

We sing, "It is well with my soul." Is that true of you this moment? Can you say, "As far as I know, there is nothing in my life that dishonors and displeases Christ"? As far as you know, every known sin is confessed and forsaken? Is that true? Then the peace of Christ does rule in your heart.

There is also an objective test. Colossians 3:16 says, *"Let the word of Christ dwell in you richly, in all wisdom; teaching and admonishing* [we saw both in chapter 1] *one another in psalms and hymns and spiritual songs, singing with grace in your hearts to the Lord."*

Musicians, the apostle Paul had a very special word for you here: "Let the word of Christ dwell in you [plural, you and your audience] richly." As Ryrie, in his inimitable style, expounds, "The psalms and hymns and spiritual songs must be both those that teach and admonish."[7] And may I add, such obedience to the Lord in this critical area will surely result in His special blessing upon such spiritual ministry.

Let me encourage you to relate every issue to the Word, as Paul does in verse 16, to determine whether it is right or wrong, to determine whether it pleases or displeases the Lord. Look for a clear principle or statement in Scripture that can be applied to the particular matter at hand.

At our house, we have found the principle of the peace of Christ in Colossians 3:15 very helpful at times in the area of guidance. We first use Romans 8:14, "For as many as are led by the Spirit of God, they are the sons of God." The Spirit of God has promised to lead. On the basis of this text, we thank Him for guidance.

Psalm 119:105 is the second principle—the Word of God: "Thy Word is a lamp unto my feet, and a light unto my path." Here we test a matter by lining it up with a principle or text of the Word.

Then, if the answer is not forthcoming, we use Colossians 3:15, "Let the peace of God rule in your hearts." We have discovered that when a course of action is God's will for us, His peace rules in our hearts. Let me encourage you to use these principles for guidance regularly. They work. They are biblical.

Our lesson in Colossians 3 has admonished us believers to deprive the members of our bodies of power when an action is wrong; that is, what displeases our Lord is to be put off, by the grace of God. And what pleases Him is to be put on, by the grace of God.

Paul then wraps it all up in verse 17, *"And whatsoever ye do in word or deed* [he doesn't leave anything out, does he?], *do all in the name of the Lord Jesus, giving thanks to God and the Father by Him."*

When we do something in the name of another, we do or act in the way that the other person would act. When we do something in the name of Jesus Christ, we do it as He would do it; we act as our Lord would act in that given situation.

In my parental home I had a brother just one year and eleven days older than I, so you know my mother had her hands full. God gave her mercy and grace. Thank you, Lord, and thank you, Mother! One day we pulled a boneheaded stunt. I won't tell you what we did! It was wrong, but we boys thought we could get away with it. Sometimes I think mothers almost possess omniscience. We were up on the bank of our cottage on a lake in upstate New York, and Mother caught us.

"Boys," she shouted, "don't you know that your mother is a Bible teacher? Don't you know that I teach Sunday school and home Bible classes? Must I give up my Bible classes because of the way you boys act?" I have never forgotten her rebuke. Of course we knew Mother could not give up her teaching. How she shamed us! We had not acted according to our name that was honorable in our community, for my parents were fine Christians.

Some years later when I was teaching in Dallas Bible College, at the close of the Lord's Day I came home from ministering, and my wife said, "You've had a phone call from one of your students."

I phoned him; then I went to minister to him. I walked in and found him drunk—a Bible college student intoxicated. He said, "Brother Gannett, I'd like for you to take me across town to the home of a friend, where I can get myself together."

As we drove through downtown Dallas on our way to Grand Prairie, he said, "Brother Gannett, I want you to stop and buy me a bottle of beer." I responded, "I cannot buy you a bottle of beer. I will not buy you a bottle of beer." He said, "In the name of Jesus Christ, I ask you to buy me a bottle of beer."

I could not buy him a bottle of beer in the name of the Lord Jesus! Anything that destroys people, one's testimony, one's body and mind, I could not do in the name of the Lord Jesus Christ, "giving thanks to God and the Father by him."

Such is the emphasis of the apostle Paul as he wrapped it all up for us, when he wrote in verse 17, "And whatsoever ye do in word or deed, do all in the name of our Lord Jesus, giving thanks to God and the Father by him."

Fellow Christian, our lesson says there is an answer to life's problems. The lesson again: Christ is the answer. Christ in the life is the One who can make you a Christlike individual, can make you a blessing to other people, can make you victorious and fruitful in your home, in your church, in your community. Trust Him, one step at a time.

Do I hear you respond, "That's what I want. I want Christ to be my life"?

He longs to be your life, my friend! He went to the cross because He loved you. He paid the supreme sacrifice—He died—on that cross for your sins, according to the Scriptures. On the third day God raised Him from the dead, according to the Scriptures. He now says to you, "For God so loved the world [including you], that He gave His only begotten Son, that whosoever [including you] believeth in Him should not perish, but have everlasting life" (John 3:16).

He will give you eternal life. He will give you grace to live a victorious life for His praise and glory. This is your opportunity to trust the Savior.

If you are looking for a reason to become a Christian, and you have children, that is sufficient reason. You have a responsibility at home in training your children. Dad, start with yourself. Mom, start by becoming an example, as Paul has enjoined.

If God has spoken to you through this Word and your heart is ready, I urge you to invite Him into your life now.

Will you pray the prayer I prayed when I was a lad? "Lord Jesus, I trust You to save me." Pray it now, where you are. "Lord, I trust You to save me."

If you prayed that prayer from your heart, He did save you. And I welcome you into the family of God. But if you are already a Christian, then start walking in union with Him, by faith. I trust that you will, right now.

Chapter 5

CHRIST THE PREEMINENT ONE

(3:18–4:18)

We turn to Colossians 3 and 4. Our theme continues that in all things He, our Lord Jesus Christ, is to be preeminent.

I trust that God has been working this grace in our lives as we have studied this grand epistle together.

We have seen His person, His work, and His ministry. We have seen how He is the answer to every false teaching. We have seen something of the practical application of our risen Lord in our personal lives.

As I write these words, my wife and I have renewed fellowship with a godly mother whose husband has insisted three times that he was going to divorce her but each time has failed to carry out his threats. She is the mother of three children, not one of whom as yet has given evidence of the preeminence of Christ in the life.

The thrilling part is that the mother is trusting God completely for her entire family. Her communication is always positive and trusting. She goes about her daily activities with a sweet, expectant spirit, and in the meantime she is trusting God to save her husband and restore him to her and the family. She still insists that she loves him dearly.

Furthermore, this kind of faith bursts forth from her personality as she serves in the marketplace, and as on Tuesday evenings she goes to the mall to share her faith in Christ with others.

With this demonstration of the reality of the truth of our text, we conclude our series on seeing Christ the preeminent One live out His life through us. He lives within us as believers and as seen in our Christian homes, as we serve in the marketplace, and as we witness to the real world about us.

Christ in the Home (3:18–21)

"Wives, submit yourselves unto your own husbands, as it is fit in the Lord. Husbands, love your wives, and be not bitter against them. Children, obey your parents in all things: for this is well pleasing unto the Lord. Fathers, provoke not your children to anger, lest they be discouraged" (vv. 18–21).

We will not take time to go into the minutiae of these verses on the Christian home, but we do want to underscore Paul's point that Christ in the life was the answer to the problems of the Colossian believers, and of ours also.

Wives (3:18)

"Submit yourselves unto your own husbands, as it is fit in the Lord." And what is that? Ephesians 5 explains that as the church is subject unto Christ, so wives are to submit themselves to their own husbands. Whenever they feel like it? No, "as it is fit in the Lord."

We are told that in the United States the divorce rate is one out of two marriages, I grieve to say. Fifty percent of the marriages are on the rocks. That need not ever happen, where the home is Christian and each member of the family is trusting Christ to live within.

When a wife is so trusting the risen Christ within, she has grace to honor God in the home, grace to submit to God-given authority in the home. No matter what the Equal Rights Amendment tells us, no matter what modern psychology teaches, this is God's way.

Are there tensions in your home? Ladies, you do not start with your husbands or children. You must start with yourselves. Wives, God says in His Word that you are to submit to your own husband as it is fit in the Lord. With Christ in your life, there is grace sufficient.

Husbands (3:19)

This is a glorious text—"love your wives." What an assignment until the Lord comes! We are to keep on loving our wives and "be not bitter against them." In the latter phrase, "the verb has the idea of being sharp, harsh, and bitter. It speaks of friction caused by impatience and thoughtless 'nagging.'" And the grammar forbids habitual action. Another has said, surely a husband's "assuming absolute authority will only embitter one's wife, not endear her." Paul writes to the Ephesians, "Let not the sun go down upon your wrath" (4:26). And earlier he admonishes the brethren to speak the truth in love (Eph. 4:15). This is "God's way of having a happy home."[1]

The verb *love* is the same as in John 3:16. This is the love that reaches out to people and says, "You are important to me. How can I minister to you and be a blessing to you?" This is the meaning here. This is divine love. When Christ is living within, the expression of that life is love.

Christ in your life will save your home, husband, when you love your wife as Christ loved the church. When a wife submits to her husband, with the husband loving the wife as Christ loved the church, the home is a God-blessed institution, by the grace of God and for the glory of God.

Children (3:20)

"Obey your parents in all things: for this is well pleasing unto the Lord." Children and young people, do you want to obey God? You do it by obeying your parents. That is where you start.

Where does a child get grace for that? He first has to be saved, led to Christ as his Savior, and then, like his parents, claim the grace of God for Christ to live within him. Christ within the child provides the grace to obey his parents. That is exactly how it works.

The only answer to the humanism in the educational system of our day—where children are taught to be free, free not to submit to authority—is God's Word. God says, "Children, obey your parents in all things: for this is well pleasing unto the Lord."

Fathers (3:21)

"Provoke not your children to anger, lest they be discouraged." Paul adds in Ephesians 6:4, "Bring them up in the nurture and admonition of the Lord."

How, when we live in such a busy day, when fathers have to spend so much time in the marketplace, can they find time to train their children? After all, many think, that is the pastor's job, the Sunday school teacher's job, the responsibility of the children's ministries. Thank God for every contribution they make. But God says, "Fathers, it's your job." Dad, we make time for what is most important, don't we?

Some years ago, I read in a management book about a counselor who walked into the office of a Pittsburgh steel magnate, the president of the company. The counselor said, "I have a great idea for you. Work on it for six weeks, and send me a check for whatever it's worth." His suggestion was: "Decide on what is most important and do it first." Six weeks later, the president of that steel corporation sent him a check for $25,000.

What is most important, Dad? You know and I know that it is our families. So we make time for our wives, don't we? And we make time for our children, don't we, by the grace of God? I trust we do. Christ in the life gives that wisdom, that grace, that discipline. You do remember, the fruit of the Spirit is love, joy, peace, and—the last one—self-control. That means a disciplined life, a life controlled by God the Holy Spirit, is possible because Christ lives within.

Christ in the Marketplace (3:22–4:1)

Paul says also that Christ in the life is the key to the marketplace, to our relationships there too. Today we call it the employer-employee relationship.

Employees (3:22–25)

Paul says, "*Servants* [employees], *obey in all things your masters according to the flesh; not with eyeservice* [clockwatchers], *as menpleasers, but in singleness* [sincerity] *of heart, fearing God. And whatever ye do, do it heartily, as to the Lord, and not unto men; knowing that of the Lord ye shall receive the reward of the inheritance: for ye serve the Lord Christ.*"

May I suggest that we would not need any unions today if we were all Spirit-filled employers and employees with Christ living within. But we are not. Most are unregenerate, non-Christians, who do not order their lives by the Scriptures.

When we were in seminary, the Mitchell Company in Dallas delighted in employing Bible college and seminary students. They knew they were not getting professional help, men and women who had been raised in the marketplace and who knew the professional skills and standards. But the company was willing to hire that type of employee in order to have a ministry of helping students through school. Throughout their manufacturing plant, over the doorways was written Colossians 3:23: "Whatever you do, do it heartily as to the Lord, and not unto men." I like that, don't you? You see, when Christ is in the life and in control, we obey in all things completely (v. 22) and do all things heartily (v. 23) to God's praise and glory.

Someone may say, "Well, Brother Gannett, you are not in the marketplace. You don't know the problems we face, everything that's unfair and irresponsible."

Verse 25 takes care of that: *"He that doeth wrong shall receive for the wrong which he hath done."* Payday is coming someday. You see, we serve the Lord Christ. There is coming a judgment seat of Christ where there will be "no respect of persons." Payday is coming, and whereas there may be a bit less in the paycheck down here, over yonder such matters will be settled fairly and justly. Christ in the life can make an employee faithful, to the glory of God.

Employers (4:1)

I had a problem, along with others, in determining budgets in Bible college administration. There was a very delicate situation with salaries. One person had an M.A. almost completed, just starting out in the teaching ministry but with great promise. What do I pay him? Here is a person with an M.A. for one or two years, another with a Master of Theology degree for four years. How do you distinguish in pay for them? Then a person who has just received a doctor's degree; another who has had one for twenty years. One is an outstanding professor, and the other is somewhat mediocre, whom you may not keep another year. Now, how do you pay that group and do it equitably?

Well, there were some answers. I am not sure I had all of them. The judgment seat of Christ will straighten it all out. And my professors then will be glorified, so they will not say, "Brother Gannett, we told you so." Down here, when Christ is living within, it is our purpose to be just and fair in the matter of remuneration for services rendered. Christ in the life gives grace for that.

Christ in Our Witness (4:2–6)

Beginning with Colossians 4:2, we turn to Christ in the life in terms of our Christian witness. *"Continue in prayer, and watch in the same with thanksgiving; withal, praying also for us, that God would open unto us a door of utterance, to speak the mystery of Christ, for which I am also in bonds: that I may make it manifest, as I ought to speak."*

We can interpret verse 2 in three different ways and possibly be accurate in all three. One is, Paul brings up the subject of prayer and emphasizes that we need to be faithful and diligent in our prayer ministry. "Continue in prayer," he says, "and watch in the same with thanksgiving"—an appropriate interpretation and application of the truth.

Paul wrote to the Thessalonians, "Pray without ceasing" (1 Thess. 5:17). Here Paul uses the same term, the strongest term in the Greek New Testament, meaning, "Keep on continuing in prayer," and then adds, "watch in the same with thanksgiving." He was saying, "Don't neglect your prayer life. Watch that you don't neglect it. Be especially careful that you don't neglect in any way this very special ministry of prayer. Be spiritually alert by praying with one eye open, if you please."

A second interpretation of this text is: "Now that we have come to the end of the epistle, I want you to get on your knees and pray, because it is in prayer that we appropriate the truth we have been teaching through this letter." That certainly is applicable here.

And while you pray, watch in the same, with thanksgiving. Be constantly alert that you are walking in union with Christ. Be constantly alert to Christ being preeminent in your life. Be alert that Christ is always all, and in all, in your life. Certainly this is a fitting application to our study together.

Because of the following verses, I want to suggest a third interpretation: our Christian witness, an appropriate note on which to conclude our theme on the preeminence of Christ.

Pray (3:2–4)

I read again verses 3 and 4: "Praying also for us, that God would open unto us a door of utterance, to speak the mystery of Christ, for which I am also in bonds: that I may make it manifest, as I ought to speak." Continue to pray, says Paul. Then he adds, "Watch in the same with thanksgiving," in relation to our witness, our testimony.

You see, spirituality is not an end in itself. Walking in union with the living Christ is not an end in itself. There is a real world out there, and most people in it are not Christians. If the Lord should come tonight, most would be left behind—an awesome fact. And so, with all the heartbeat of the Son of God, with all Christ is and what He accomplished at Calvary, Paul is saying, "Pray about all this!"

What do you pray about when you pray regarding your Christian witness? In verse 3 Paul suggests that we pray for more opportunity to witness. Remember, Paul was a prisoner in Rome when he wrote this letter, and he pleaded with his readers to pray that a door of utterance would be opened for him to speak the mystery of Christ and to share the gospel with clarity (v. 4), as he ought to speak.

Paul is saying, "I want to be the most effective witness possible in this prison, in terms of redeeming every opportunity and ministering my Lord with clarity, so that the greatest number will come to know Jesus Christ as Savior and Lord." He pleads, "Pray with me about this."

Do you pray about soul winning in your own life? Do you pray for opportunities to witness? For greater clarity in witness?

Wendell P. Loveless, who wrote the music for the gospel chorus, "Lord, lay some soul upon my heart, and love that soul through me," said in my hearing at a Bible conference some years ago, "Every morning I ask God for at least two opportunities to share Jesus Christ with others." He was praying for opportunities to witness to people.

Do you pray about knowing the Word better, so that you can witness better—with greater clarity? Also, that hard soil, thin soil, and dirty soil will become good soil (Matt. 13), so that as you sow the Word of God and water it, God will in fact bring the increase, to His praise and glory.

We are to pray about the preparation of our own hearts, for the leadership of the Holy Spirit to bring someone across our path, so that we will have the opportunity to share Christ to one who needs our wonderful Savior.

Do you do much praying about this in your midweek service in your church? Prayer is important because it is emphasized all through the Bible. Prayer is God's appointed way of getting things (Matt. 7:7–11). How displeased God must be when as church members, some of us can go all week and not take time to pray. We are to pray for one another, pray for our missionaries, pray for our leadership, pray for our witness in the community. We are to pray about evangelism.

Walk (3:5)

Verse 5 emphasizes our walk, our daily testimony. *"Walk in wisdom toward them that are without* [that is, outside the family of God], *redeeming the time* [the opportunities]." This is what we call lifestyle evangelism.

Our Lord gave it to us in the Sermon on the Mount. He used the terms *salt* and *light*. We are the salt of the earth, and the salt is not to lose its savor. We are to be the light of the world and not put our light under a bushel. We should let the world see our wonderful Lord. We are to let our light so shine that men may see our good works and glorify our Father who is in heaven.

As we know, most of the unsaved will not come to church. Most of them will not read the Bible. They will not listen to the gospel on radio and television. So you and I are the only version of the Word most people see. Does there need to be a revised version in your life and in mine? Do they see Christ in us—the glory, the beauty, the wonder, the loveliness of Christ living through you and me in every relationship every day?

In his book about lifestyle evangelism, Joseph Aldrich, the president of Multnomah Bible College, said, "Edification is the key to evangelism." You see, when we are indeed edified and growing and maturing in Christ and are becoming more Christlike, we are then the lifestyle witness that will attract people to our wonderful Savior.

Ladies, do you remember how you used to work at catching your man? (You don't confess to that at all, do you?) We men remember so well how we felt when we were not sure where we stood. Whatever we thought would do the job, we worked at it, didn't we? Whatever it took, we worked at it.

How are we going to win a world? By working at it. First, by being Christlike, by loving with the love of Christ, by expressing in our lives the resurrected life of the Lord Jesus Christ—throughout every day, every week, every month, every year. We make Christ attractive to the unsaved, who hurt and are miserable and are going to hell without Christ.

A lifestyle Christian witness is someone who has reality, someone who has love, someone who is genuine, someone who does not have to live on the gimmicks, the drugs, the liquor, the sex, and all that goes on today. Here is someone who is pure and clean and honorable before God and men, who does an honest day's work for an honest day's pay, who serves God and loves people. Is that what is different about you?

I heard the story about a young lad selling apples on a train. The price was only a nickel, so you know this story is many years old, but the principle is as up-to-date as this hour.

He walked through the car saying, "Apple?" And the reply came, "No." "Apple?" Another negative response. "Apple?" "No, thanks." He went all the way to the end of the car and did not sell even one apple. Then he returned dejectedly and took his seat.

A wise old salesman said, "Son, here is a nickel. I want one of your apples, and I want to help you sell the rest. I will go up to the front of the car, and I want you to keep your eye on me. When I wink, go through the car again selling your apples."

So the salesman went and stood at the front of the car. He held up the apple, took a handkerchief out, and began to polish that apple. He leisurely polished it and then polished it some more. Finally he decided it was time to take out his pocket knife, and he stood there leaning against the door peeling the apple. The peelings fell on the floor at his feet. Then he took his knife and cut out one slice of the apple and put it in his mouth. He stood there, throughly enjoying chewing that juicy apple. Then he winked at the boy.

The boy started down the aisle again, calling out, "Apple?" "Yes sir!" came the first response. "Apple, mister?" "Yes sir!" said the next. "Apple?" "Yes sir!" And he emptied the bag. What made the difference? The apples were now attractive.

The world out there is full of sin, wickedness, and debauchery, and what it needs is something delightfully different, and that is found in our Lord Jesus Christ. So Paul said, "Walk. As ye have received Christ Jesus the Lord, walk in union with Him."

Talk (3:6)

What else? *"Let your speech be always with grace, seasoned with salt, that ye may know how ye ought to answer every man."*

Here are three means, and to my knowledge the only three means in all the Bible, for reaching people for Christ: *Pray. Walk. Talk.*

Paul said that we are to let our speech be always with grace. Our speech is not always with grace. Is that true of you? A lot of speech does not attract people to Jesus Christ. We are to be gracious. Christ in the life adds that grace.

We are to be salt. What does salt do? (It gives high blood pressure!) Salt is seasoning. It makes food taste better, brings out the flavor. Salt in the life makes the Christian life tastier, so to speak.

Salt preserves. I am old enough to remember going down to the cellar to a crock of salt brine and bringing up some eggs for Mother to cook for breakfast. Salt preserves. The grace of God within us preserves our Christian testimony and makes it effective.

To what end? "That ye may know how ye ought to answer every man." The inference is that people ask about Christ. In his first epistle, Peter puts it this way: "Sanctify the Lord God in your hearts: and be ready always to give an answer to every man that asketh you a reason for the hope that is in you with meekness and fear" (3:15). Most people do not come up to you and say, "I want to be a Christian. Please tell me how."

I remember interviewing a woman for the position of Dean of Women at Southeastern Bible College some years ago. I said, "We are a nondenominational school, so we do not require that you be a member of a certain denomination. But we want to know that you are saved and that you walk with the Lord. Please give me your testimony."

She told about attending a university nearby. She said that during her first year she befriended a sophomore, and that the sophomore had something she did not have. All year long she noticed the godliness and Christlikeness of this friend.

She returned for her second year and said to this same friend, "Tell me. Am I a Christian?" Her fellow student's response was, "Well, I don't know. I am not in the business of telling people whether they are saved or not." The first girl said, "But you have something I don't have, and I want to know what it is."

Most of the time when people want to know about Christ, it is couched in a circuitous conversation. They talk about church. They talk about their children having problems, and thus they are setting up a context for us to offer the solution to their problems. The solution is found in our Lord Jesus Christ.

Fellow Christian, we need to cultivate the sensitivity of being alert when people bring up the subject of the things of God. In fact, they are often seeking the Lord, but they do not verbalize it directly. Talk is essential! Paul reminds us, "Faith cometh by hearing, and hearing by the Word of God" (Rom. 10:17).

With all the prayer, and with all the Christlike living, there must come a time when we tell them of the Lord Jesus Christ, that they may be "born again not of corruptible seed, but of incorruptible, by the word of God, which liveth and abideth forever" (1 Peter 1:23). Someone must share the Word of God— someone must talk.

The time comes when we should give our testimony, and it does not take Bible college or seminary education to do that. We can give them a simple verse like John 3:16, or Romans 3:23 or 6:23. We need to have memorized key verses that we can share.

The time comes when our presence is not enough; they must hear the Word of the Lord in order to be saved. This is a challenge to me to know my Bible better, to memorize the great texts of Scripture that I can use without even a New Testament in my hand, when the subject of the gospel comes up and I have the opportunity to lead a friend to the Savior.

Again, there are three ways, and only three, to lead a person to Christ. Remember these three words: *Pray. Walk. Talk.*

Conclusion *(4:12–18)*

In general, the closing part of this letter contains a few brief words for the believers at Colosse and Laodicea and a final greeting.

I want to use three verses in conclusion. *"Epaphras, who is one of you, a servant of Christ, saluteth* [greeteth] *you, always laboring fervently for you in prayers, that ye may stand perfect and complete in all the will of God"* (v. 12).

"Say to Archippus, Take heed to the ministry which thou hast received in the Lord, that thou fulfil it" (v. 17). And finally, verse 18, *"Grace be with you. Amen."*

That is God's ministry for you. I hope it is clear after this series of studies. Whatever God has called you to do, by God's grace do it. Exercise the spiritual gifts He has given you. Do the witnessing He has given you to do. Live the life He has instructed you to live. And let me share it once more, "As ye have received Christ Jesus the Lord, so walk ye in [union with] him." In all things, let Him be the preeminent One.

Two Personal Questions

First, let me ask you a personal question: Is Christ first in your life? If you have to confess in the presence of God that He is not, I beg you to repent.

If Christ is not first, confess whatever is the usurper, whatever it is that has become an idol in your life—a person, a job, an ambition. Confess those sins to the Lord, and give Christ the preeminent place in your life.

Will you now humble yourself, bow the knee, and crown Christ *Lord*? Will you do that now, with all your heart?

Did you think at the beginning of this study that you were a Christian but you now realize, after studying this Word of God, that you are not? Then you need to be saved before you go back into the real world tomorrow. Will you trust Christ now? Again, here is the prayer I prayed as a child: "Lord Jesus, I trust You to save me." Will you pray that from your heart right now? Take a moment and do it.

If you just did, thank Him! If you meant it, He has just saved you. You have the assurance, the authority of the Word of God in Romans 10:13, "For whosoever shall call upon the name of the Lord shall be saved."

"The Lord Jesus Christ is all we need, for He is the all-sufficient Christ."[2]

Christ preeminent!

Notes

Chapter 1

1. W. Graham Scroggie, *Know Your Bible,* 2 vols. (London: Pickering & Inglis, 1940), 2:187–90.
2. F. F. Bruce, *The Epistle to the Colossians, to Philemon, and to the Ephesians,* New International Commentary on the New Testament (Grand Rapids: Eerdmans, 1984), 47.
3. Ibid.
4. W. H. Griffith Thomas, *The Apostle Peter, Outline Studies of His Life, Character, and Writings* (Grand Rapids: Eerdmans, 1946), 179.

Chapter 2

1. W. Graham Scroggie, *Know Your Bible,* 2 vols. (London: Pickering & Inglis, 1940), 2:193–94.
2. S. Lewis Johnson Jr., "Christ Preeminent," *Bibliotheca Sacra* 119 (January–March 1962), 13.
3. H. A. Ironside, *Lectures on the Epistle to the Colossians* (New York: Loizeaux Brothers, 1928), 46.
4. S. Lewis Johnson Jr., "From Enmity to Amity," *Bibliotheca Sacra* 120 (April–June 1962), 140.
5. Ibid., 142.
6. Ibid.
7. Robert G. Gromacki, *Stand Perfect in Wisdom: An Exposition of Colossians and Philemon* (Grand Rapids: Baker, 1978), 74.
8. Warren W. Wiersbe, "Philippians," *The Bible Exposition Commentary,* 2 vols. (Wheaton: Victor Books, 1989), 2:76.

9. John Eadie, *Commentary on the Epistle of Paul to the Colossians* (1856; Grand Rapids: Zondervan, 1957).
10. Johnson, "From Enmity to Amity," 145.
11. Homer A. Kent Jr., *Treasures of Wisdom: Studies in Colossians and Philemon,* New Testament Studies (Grand Rapids: Baker, 1978), 57.
12. William Hendriksen, *Exposition of Colossians and Philemon,* New Testament Commentary (Grand Rapids: Baker, 1973), 85.
13. Robert L. Saucy, *The Church in God's Program* (Chicago: Moody Press, 1972), 60.
14. C. C. Ryrie, *The Ryrie Study Bible* (Chicago: Moody Press, 1976), note on Colossians 1:26.
15. C. C. Ryrie, *Balancing the Christian Life* (Chicago: Moody Press, 1972), 159.

Chapter 3

1. C. C. Ryrie, *The Ryrie Study Bible* (Chicago: Moody Press, 1972), note on Colossians 2:9.
2. Curtis Vaughn, "Colossians," in vol. 2 of *The Expositor's Bible Commentary,* ed. Frank E. Gaebelein (Grand Rapids: Regency Reference Library, 1978), 199.
3. Robert G. Gromacki, *Stand Perfect in Wisdom: An Exposition of Colossians and Philemon* (Grand Rapids: Baker, 1978), 108.
4. S. Lewis Johnson Jr., "The Paralysis of Legalism," *Bibliotheca Sacra* 120 (April–June 1963), 112.
5. Warren W. Wiersbe, "Colossians," *The Bible Exposition Commentary,* 2 vols. (Wheaton: Victor Books, 1989), 2:130.
6. Gromacki, *Stand Perfect in Wisdom,* 121.
7. William Hendriksen, *Exposition of Colossians and Philemon,* New Testament Commentary (Grand Rapids: Baker, 1973), 128.

Chapter 4

1. Homer A. Kent Jr., *Treasures of Wisdom: Studies in Colossians and Philemon,* New Testament Studies (Grand Rapids: Baker, 1978), 117.
2. Renald E. Showers, *The New Nature* (Neptune, N.J.: Loizeaux Brothers, 1986), 123–24. Note with Showers that the old man is defined as the unregenerate man or human person in his unregenerate state. The new man is defined as the regenerate man or human person in his regenerate state. The new man, according to Colossians 3:10, experiences a renewal but not the new disposition: "The law of God is written in the heart of the regenerate man. Thus, the new disposition is in the human person, but is not the new man."
3. Warren W. Wiersbe, "Colossians," *The Bible Exposition Commentary,* 2 vols. (Wheaton: Victor Books, 1987), 2:136.
4. Robert G. Gromacki, *Stand Perfect in Wisdom: An Exposition of Colossians and Philemon* (Grand Rapids: Baker, 1978), 117.
5. Fritz Rienecker, *Linguistic Key to the Greek New Testament,* ed. Cleon L. Rogers Jr. (Grand Rapids: Regency Reference Library, 1976), 580.
6. S. Lewis Johnson Jr., "Christian Apparel," *Bibliotheca Sacra* 121 (January–March 1964), 30.
7. C. C. Ryrie, *The Ryrie Study Bible* (Chicago: Moody Press, 1976), note on Colossians 3:16.

Chapter 5

1. Fritz Rienecker, *Linguistic Key to the Greek New Testament,* ed. Cleon L. Rogers Jr. (Grand Rapids: Regency Reference Library, 1976), 582.
2. Theodore H. Epp, *The All-Sufficient Christ: Studies in Colossians* (Lincoln, Neb.: Back to the Bible, 1989), 179.

More Helpful Works on Colossians

COLOSSIANS
Where Life Is Established
by Roy L. Laurin

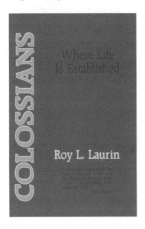

"I have read every book Roy Laurin has ever written."
—Billy Graham

This practical study on Colossians encourages Christian living on the basis of truth and action, as explained in Paul's epistle. This devotional commentary reminds us that the issues of life and truth must be continually pursued and applied.

ISBN 0-8254-3135-2   **192 pp.**

STUDIES IN COLOSSIANS AND PHILEMON
by W. H. Griffith Thomas

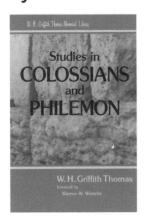

"One of the best expositions available, not only for the advanced student, but also for the average reader who wants to gain a working knowledge of this material."
—Warren W. Wiersbe

This excellent homiletical material, together with informative outlines, gives the reader rich insight and practical knowledge in the study of Colossians and Philemon. Two appendixes on the life and work of Paul and a general survey of Paul's epistles complement this book.

ISBN 0-8254-3834-9   192 pp.

William Ramsay's Studies in the New Testament

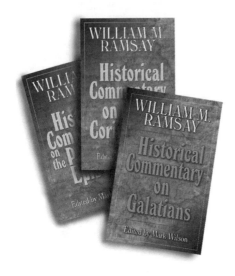

As a writer and scholar whose career spanned the latter part of the nineteenth century and the early twentieth century, Sir William Ramsay's keen insights into first-century culture and geography have always been valued by biblical scholars of succeeding generations.

Now for the first time in book form, Ramsay's series of articles on First Corinthians and the Pastoral Epistles are once again available. The original studies, which appeared in *The Sunday School Times* in 1909 and 1911, have been prepared for publication by Mark Wilson, Adjunct Professor of New Testament at Regent University, Virginia Beach, Virginia. The text of all three works has been edited for continuity and changes in terminology without altering the essential content of Ramsay's work.

Historical Commentary on the Pastoral Epistles
ISBN 0-8254-3636-2   **160 pp.**

Historical Commentary on First Corinthians
ISBN 0-8254-3637-0   **176 pp.**

Historical Commentary on Galatians
ISBN 0-8254-3638-9   **368 pp.**